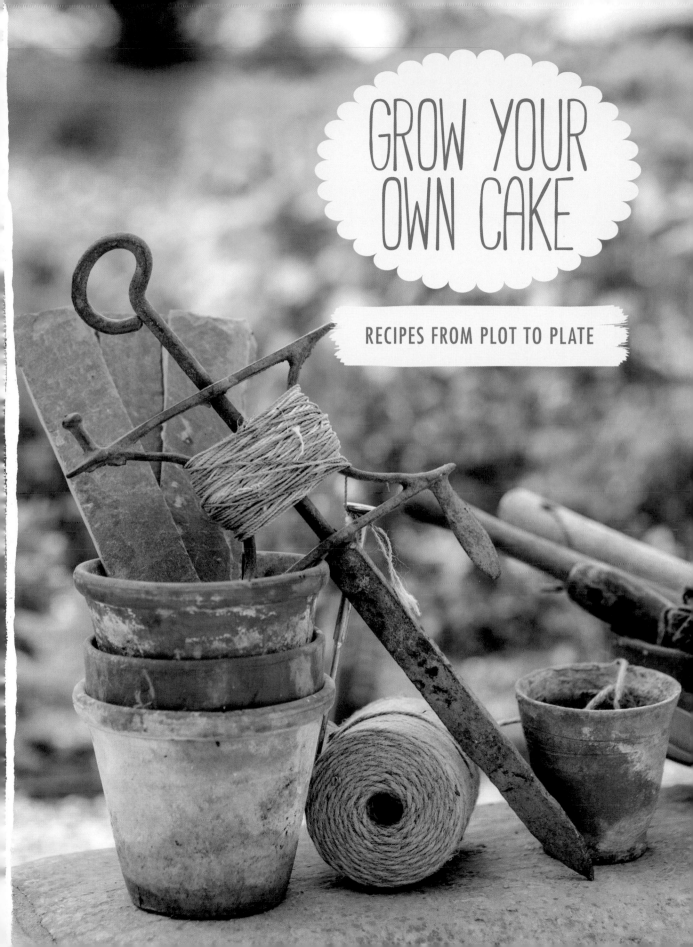

GROW YOUR OWN CAKE

RECIPES FROM PLOT TO PLATE

GROW YOUR OWN CAKE

RECIPES FROM PLOT TO PLATE

HOLLY FARRELL

PHOTOGRAPHS BY JASON INGRAM

FRANCES LINCOLN

To Felicity

Frances Lincoln Limited
74–77 White Lion Street
London N1 9PF

Grow Your Own Cake
Copyright © Frances Lincoln
   Limited 2016
Text copyright ©
   Holly Farrell 2016
Photographs copyright ©
   Jason Ingram 2016
   except those listed on p176
Design by Becky Clarke Design

First Frances Lincoln edition
2016

A catalogue record for this
book is available from the
British Library.

ISBN 978-0-7112-3701-8

Printed and bound in China

9 8 7 6 5 4 3 2 1

Quarto is the authority on a wide
range of topics.

Quarto educates, entertains
and enriches the lives of our
readers – enthusiasts and lovers
of hands-on living.

www.QuartoKnows.com

CONTENTS

INTRODUCTION

I have yet to meet a gardener who was not happy to sit down with a cup of tea and a slice of cake. Yet beyond the classics – carrot cake, and the inevitable 'I've got a glut of courgettes, I know, I will bake them in a cake' courgette cake – vegetables do not tend to feature in baking very often. Fruit, being obviously sweeter, is a different matter, although even then it tends to be reserved for puddings rather than cakes. I have therefore taken the best of the veg patch and fruit cage – and the herb and flower gardens too – and celebrated them in baked form.

One of the perennial arguments about growing your own vegetables (and fruit) is do they actually taste better than the produce in the shops? Well, the way I see it, the fresher something is and the longer it has had to ripen on the plant, the better it will taste. Plus, if you grow your own, you can try, test and choose the varieties you prefer, rather than being slave to the supermarkets' choices, which are usually dictated more by shelf life and how well that fruit or vegetable travels rather than by any consideration for flavour. You also get the opportunity to try many things that are simply not available in the shops, or are at least very difficult to find and very expensive, such as fresh rose flowers, lemon verbena leaves or fresh borlotti beans. Finally, although there is no scientific way of proving it, the satisfaction of eating something you have grown yourself makes it taste ten times better.

If gardening is about contentment with the simple life, baking should be too. Although obviously you want your bakes to look good, it is the effort you put into them that matters more to the person you are baking for. So what if your sponge is a little lopsided, or the icing was a bit runny, or the fig juice leaked into the custard? No one's going to notice, and if they do they should not care because you have just baked them a cake. (The exception to this of course is when you are baking competitively.) Baking cakes is fun, and eating them is even better; there is more to life than perfect frosting.

With that in mind I have endeavoured to keep things simple and natural in *Grow Your Own Cake*. I find recipes that call for tiny amounts of ten different obscure ingredients rather annoying: it means I cannot bake the cake on a whim, because I have to go and source all those ingredients, and I am then left with ten open packets of things I am unlikely to use again for a while clogging up the cupboard. So, to bake all the cakes in this book you need only a few different cake tins, and hardly any of the recipes call for uncommon ingredients.

If you have flour, eggs, butter, sugar and a few store-cupboard staples you should be able to walk into the kitchen with some freshly picked fruit or vegetable and bake it into something delicious.

It is time for the bad news. Unfortunately, despite containing a good proportion of fruit and veg, I cannot claim these bakes are healthy. They are still cakes and puddings at the end of the day. However (and this is in no way scientifically proven) you must burn some of the calories in the cake when you cultivate the ingredients, so that has got to be a good reason to grow your own cake.

I would encourage you to be realistic in your ambitions if you are new to gardening. It is very (*very*) easy to get carried away with seed catalogues and online plant shopping, so before you begin be brutal in your assessment of how much time you have to dedicate to your plot. The best thing to do is to start small – a couple of pots of herbs on the windowsill for example – and scale up from there, rather than launching gung-ho into an overambitious project that becomes a daunting nightmare, a burden rather than a joy. Yes, I would love you to be growing a huge range of fruit, vegetables, herbs and flowers, because I think gardening is brilliant, but I would also like you to be enjoying yourself.

If you are already a baker, growing your own fruit and vegetables allows you to produce spectacular and unusual cakes to impress your friends. Some are already classics, such as carrot cake (see page 52), apple pie (see page 138) and beetroot brownies (see page 108), while others are more unusual, such as fennel cake (see page 70) and pea cheesecake (see page 160). If you are already a gardener, growing your own does not have to mean rows of potatoes and onions when you can use your produce in cakes and bakes. If you are neither a baker nor a gardener, well hopefully I will inspire you to take up both pastimes.

GROW IT, BAKE IT, EAT IT.

USING THIS BOOK

The two introductory chapters, *In the Garden* and *In the Kitchen*, contain all the general information you will need to get started. Terms and techniques used in the Grow and Bake pages such as 'sow thinly' or 'make the pastry' are explained too.

Each crop has its own Grow page, and each recipe a Bake page. First come the larger cakes, divided by season: Spring & Summer Cakes, and Autumn & Winter Cakes. Such an arrangement should not deter you from delving into an out-of-season chapter if you have the appropriate fruit or vegetables to hand. Afternoon Tea contains most of the smaller bakes suitable for that occasion, while Puddings has dessert cakes, tarts and cheesecake for every time of year. Finally Savoury Bakes such as simple breads and tarts offer the chance of serving a home-grown main course as well.

A NOTE ON THE RECIPES

When weighing out ingredients, use the metric or the imperial measures – never mix the two systems.

See *In the Kitchen* for more information but unless otherwise stated:

- Oven temperatures in degrees Celsius/ Fahrenheit are for fan ovens. Add 20°C/50°F if you do not have a fan oven.
- Vegetables and fruit are washed, scrubbed and topped-and-tailed as appropriate.
- All ingredients, especially butter and eggs, are used at room temperature.
- Eggs are medium size.

BAKING WITH ALLERGIES & INTOLERANCES

The following recipes are wheat-free (WF), gluten-free (GF), dairy-free (DF) or dairy-free without the frosting:

- Beetroot cake (see page 60) DF;
- Blackcurrant mini-pavlovas (see page 132) WF/GF;
- Carrot & almond cake (see page 51) WF/GF/DF without frosting;
- Chocolate & raspberry bean cake (see page 68) WF/GF/DF;
- Flower meringues (see page 126) WF/GF/DF;
- Hazelnut & rosemary pavlova (see page 153) WF/GF;
- Pea cheesecake (see page 160) WF;
- Poppy seed flower-pot bread (see page 157) DF;
- Tomato cupcakes (see page 117) DF without frosting.

All the recipes involving pastry can be made gluten-free, see page 38.

IN THE GARDEN

Many people are convinced they do not have 'green fingers', and that any plant they attempt to grow will wilt before their eyes. This is simply not true. Plants do not have feelings; they cannot fail to flourish out of spite. They are biologically programmed to grow and flower and all you need do is provide each one with a few basics: something to grow in, some light and some water. The plant will do the rest.

Below I have given some general tips for successful growing and have explained some basic procedures that are common to many crops, such as how to sow seeds.

BUYING PLANTS & SEEDS

Purchasing seeds from a reputable seed merchant is relatively risk-free, as they are bound by regulations to ensure a high proportion of the seed will germinate if sown correctly. Do make sure that they are within their sow-by date, because many seeds lose viability after a year or so.

Plant buying is much more a case of *caveat emptor* (buyer beware). If you are doing this online, use only trustworthy suppliers (**SEE PAGE 171** for some recommendations) or sites that offer a no-quibbles return policy. When choosing plants in a shop, do not be afraid to give each one a good check over before you part with your cash. Some retailers may sell some poor-quality plants. Run down this checklist in your head:

- Is it the right time of year to be buying this plant? This applies especially to young vegetable plants sold in trays.

LEFT A string line is useful to mark out where to sow your row of seeds.

ABOVE Although the right-hand tomato plant is taller and has some fruit on it, the left-hand plant is healthier, sturdier and a better choice.

Although they will not survive a frost if planted outside, garden centres begin to stock plants such as climbing beans in early spring, which is several months before they can be safely put in open ground.

- Does the plant look healthy? Are the leaves green and full, or yellowing and wilted (and so better avoided)? Is it covered in pests and does it look diseased?
- Is it (if applicable) a well-branched plant, or a puny stick? Short, stocky plants are always a better choice than tall, thin ones.
- If the plant is bare-root, do the roots look

ABOVE A root-bound lemon verbena (left) and the better choice plant (right) that has grown well in its pot.

ABOVE A lot of loose compost will fall out of a recently potted-on plant; always check what is in the pot before you buy.

healthy and are there plenty of them? Bare-root plants do not have much more than their large, woody roots, but these should be strong enough to anchor the plant in the soil.

- If growing in a pot, turn the plant out to look at its root ball. It should have roots that extend into all of the compost, but have not gone round and round the inside of the pot (that is, be root-bound). If a lot of loose compost falls out (mind your shoes) to reveal a smaller root ball, it has been recently potted-on into that larger pot, and you would be paying a lot more money for a bit of empty compost.

SEE ALSO *Plant names.*

COMPOST

Technically, compost is the organic matter you would make yourself, by rotting down plant material over a year or so until it has turned into a nutrient-rich, soil-like substance that can be dug into or spread over the top of the beds to improve the soil quality. However the word compost is also widely used to describe the various types of soil-substitutes available to buy in bags to fill pots and sow seeds in.

When buying compost, consider what you need it for. To plant up pots, multipurpose compost is fine, unless you are growing blueberries or cranberries, in which case you will need ericaceous compost. This has an acidic pH, and is often marketed as rhododendron and camellia compost. For sowing seeds, you will require a finer-grade medium, so buy the specific seed compost.

There are also environmental considerations. Organic compost, which is free from pesticides and herbicides, is

available if you prefer to use that. Many composts are now also peat-free, although sometimes the environmental impact of the substitutes used is almost as bad as the peat. In general you get what you pay for, so buy the best quality you can afford.
SEE ALSO *Organic matter*.

CUTTING BACK

Plants whose top growth dies back over winter to shoot anew in spring need the dead growth cutting back. This can be done in autumn or winter – in fact any time before the new shoots start appearing – and if the stems are left to stand over winter they will provide shelter for beneficial insects such as ladybirds. Whenever you tackle this job, cut off the dead stems back to ground level.

DIGGING & PREPARING SOIL

To dig or not to dig? That is the question I am sure Hamlet would have asked if he spent more time in the garden and less time moping about the castle. The arguments for and against are, essentially, this:

- Digging over vegetable beds every year allows for the incorporation of organic matter (SEE *Organic matter*) and the removal of perennial weed roots; it also relieves compaction. However it brings more weed seeds to the surface where they can then germinate.
- Not digging, that is, just spreading on a layer of mulch every autumn and raking over the area before planting and sowing in spring, preserves the balance of the soil's structure and ecosystems, allowing all the soil flora and fauna to do the work of incorporating the organic matter and keeping the soil aerated for you. However this takes time and will not help a compacted soil in the short term.

Personally I favour a mix of the two approaches: spread a good, thick layer of mulch over the beds in autumn, then in spring use a garden fork to turn the soil over gently, not going too deep, but levering it up slightly. On first creating a new bed I would always dig it over properly (not forgetting to add plenty of organic matter), as the soil is likely to be quite compacted and weedy. Once dug, or not, use a rake to break down smaller clumps of soil or organic matter on the surface, remove larger stones and create a level surface.

DISEASES

Most plant diseases are fungal rots that start on a single leaf or wounded part of the plant and spread from there. This means that they are easy to prevent. Keep plants healthy to enable them to fight off disease more effectively. Use clean pots and tools; buy healthy plants; do not set plants too close together (humidity and poor air circulation foster fungi); and remove any diseased parts with a clean cut back to healthy growth.
SEE PAGE 171 for sources of information to deal with specific problems.

EQUIPMENT

You do not need a lot of fancy equipment to start growing plants. These basics will meet your needs, initially at least:

- trowel for planting small plants and/or shovelling compost into a pot;
- hand fork for weeding;
- spade and/or garden fork for digging over the soil (if you have any) and for planting trees and other large plants;
- large rake for preparing the soil (if you have any);
- seed trays and/or small pots in which to sow seeds;
- pots into which to plant (if you are using containers);
- compost for planting up pots and sowing seeds (SEE *Compost*);
- watering can;
- secateurs for cutting woody stems – for softer, smaller plants kitchen scissors are adequate.

FERTILIZERS

Plants can get most of their nutrients from the soil, water and air, but sometimes need a little extra. For example, those grown in pots will exhaust the nutrients in the potting compost within a few months, and vegetables are hungry crops, having to do a lot in the short time they have to get to harvestable size, so a little extra nutrition will not go amiss there either. The application of fertilizer to plants is often called 'feeding'.

Liquid fertilizers are short-term, fast-action and the most expensive way to feed your plants. There are many types available, including multipurpose vegetable and fruit feed, seaweed extract and specific flowering and fruiting fertilizers such as tomato feed. All contain the three main nutrients of nitrogen (N), phosphorus (P) and potassium/ kalium (K) in varying ratios. A balanced fertilizer, which is good for regular feeding of container-grown plants, will have these three in roughly equal proportions (look for the N:P:K ratio on the packet) as well as a range of other nutrients. Tomato fertilizers will have a much higher proportion of potassium/ kalium, and are good to use once a crop has started to produce flowers and fruit.

Alternatively granular, slower-acting fertilizers are available and these are applied around the base of the plant. Their nutrients are released as the granules dissolve and therefore last longer.

Whether you choose liquid or granular fertilizers, always follow the instructions on the packet, and do not exceed the recommended dosage. You need to apply fertilizer only through the growing season (spring to late summer).

HARDENING OFF

Plants raised (from seed) indoors must be hardened off before they can be put outside; if this is not done, the sudden drop in temperature will be a shock and delay their growth. Acclimatize plants over the course of a week by moving them outside just in the daytime at first, then overnight with a covering of horticultural fleece or newspaper, then finally leave them uncovered at night. They are then ready to plant out (if applicable). Of course if you have a cold frame in which to harden off your plants, this is ideal, and its closable roof replaces the need for fleece or newspaper at night.

MULCH

Mulch is any kind of organic matter (**SEE** *Organic matter*) that is applied over the surface of the soil or around the base of a plant (and 'mulching' is its application). Mulches are generally applied annually in spring, to add nutrients, conserve soil moisture and improve soil structure (they will gradually be incorporated into the soil by worms).

Ensure the soil is moist (water it if necessary), then spread a 2–3cm/¾–1¼in-thick layer over the soil, taking care not to let it actually touch the stems or trunks of plants. **SEE ALSO** *Soil*.

ORGANIC MATTER

Organic matter is any kind of plant or animal waste that is used as a mulch or dug into the soil to enrich it. It is not necessarily free from pesticides and herbicides. Before being added to the soil, any organic matter should be well-rotted: for example, horse manure needs to be left for at least a couple of years. When the organic matter is crumbly, dark brown and sweet-smelling it is ready to use.

PESTS

Unfortunately the animal kingdom does not appreciate that you want to be repaid with a harvest for the investment and effort you put into your crops, and pests will readily come and eat them before you get the chance. However there are a number

RIGHT Cold frames are ideal for hardening off plants.

of things you can do to reduce the risk and limit the damage done by pests.

As with plant diseases, practising good plant hygiene helps keep plants healthy. If they are also watered, fed and otherwise well looked after, they will be strong and better able to withstand attacks by insects such as aphids (blackfly and greenfly). Keeping weeds down also reduces pests' hiding places.

Watch your plants attentively as you tend them: turn over the leaves and check the undersides; assess their general appearance; and move pots and check under their rims to seek out snoozing slugs (slugs will be on the move at dusk and dawn, and this is the best time to catch them). A pest infestation caught and removed early will save a lot of remedial effort later. Protecting your crops with netting or other structures is not attractive, but sometimes the only way to deter pests. Red fruit is a magnet to birds, and netting your soft fruit plants may be necessary while they are ripening.

Finally get help from nature. A diverse, vibrant patch, with plenty of flowers and different plants, will attract not only the pollinators you need but also insects such as hoverflies and ladybirds, whose larvae feed on aphids. A small pond, if you can make one, could attract frogs and toads, who love to lunch on slugs. Birds will eat snails as well as your fruit, so provide winter food and water for them too.

SEE PAGE 171 for sources of information to deal with specific problems.

PLANT NAMES

Every plant has a Latin name that is unique to it. Many also have a common name, but these vary so much across regions and countries that it would be difficult to know whether you were buying the plant you actually wanted. The only way to be sure is to check its Latin name. To use Latin names you do not require an in-depth understanding of the naming system. Just be aware that all plant names have two parts (genus and species), and then potentially a variety (or cultivar, short for cultivated variety) name as well. For example, *Lavandula angustifolia* is the two-part name for the type of lavender that is delicious in shortbread (SEE PAGE 128). If you asked for just 'lavender', you could end up with *Lavandula stoechas*, which is poisonous. Then, if you wanted a particularly compact plant, you might want to get the cultivar 'Hidcote', so you would therefore need *Lavandula angustifolia* 'Hidcote'.

Fruit and vegetables are the exception to this rule – all have Latin names of course, but the common names are much more widely used. Here too there are many different varieties, but they are generally sold as, for example, apple 'Bramley's Seedling' rather than *Malus domestica* 'Bramley's Seedling'.

PLANTING

When planting a tree, shrub or other type of plant into the ground, follow the same steps regardless of its size and whether it is bare-root or potted.

Planting is best done in spring and autumn, when the soil is warm and there is usually plenty of rain. Be prepared to water (perhaps even twice daily) anything planted in hot weather. It is also possible to plant in winter, but the plants are generally dormant, and will not put on much root or shoot growth until spring.

Prepare the soil thoroughly before planting by digging over the area (a radius of 50cm/20in from where the plant will go if you can) to relieve any compaction and enable the roots to spread easily through the soil. You get only one chance to do this, so do it well. Do not turn the soil over more than you have to; just break up the clods and remove any weeds (a garden fork is often

LEFT Mint can be planted (plunged) together with its pot to avoid its roots taking over the entire bed.

better than a spade for this). Then dig the hole for the plant. It should be the same depth as the root ball on the plant, so that the crown is flush with soil level, and the planting hole should be twice as wide as the root ball. Use a fork to break up the soil in the bottom of the hole. Water the bottom of the hole (with a full large watering can). Put the plant in the hole and backfill around it, firming it in quite vigorously. You should not be able to pull it out of the soil if you give the stem a quick tug. Water the plant again (this will also help to bed it in), and spread some mulch (**SEE** *Mulch*) around the base.

Until the plant is able to grow new roots into the soil in search of water and food, it is reliant on what it can take up from the root ball – it is therefore still essentially in a pot. Water it frequently for at least two weeks, until it shows signs of significant new growth, indicating it has also put out new roots. Continue to keep an eye on the plant in hot weather though.
SEE ALSO *Planting out.*

ABOVE Take a plug plant out of its tray by pulling on a leaf and squeezing the tray underneath.

PLANTING OUT

Planting out is the term used to describe the steps by which young (plug) plants, raised from seed (usually indoors) and hardened off, are planted out into the ground or larger pots outside. Water the plugs before planting. Prepare and rake the soil (**SEE** *Digging*), then use a trowel to dig a small hole for the plant. Put it into the hole so the top of the plug-shaped root ball is at soil level, and firm the soil around it. Take care not to press down directly around the stem. Water in well.
SEE ALSO *Planting.*

PLUG PLANTS

Plug plants (also known as module-grown or module plants) are young seedlings raised in a modular tray (**SEE** *Sowing seeds*), resulting in a plug-shaped root ball. Individual plug seedlings are much easier to plant than seedlings sown all in one tray. To remove a plug plant from its tray, hold a leaf – never the delicate stem – between thumb and forefinger. Use the other hand to squeeze the plastic cell around the root ball (or push up through the cell hole in the base of a polystyrene tray), thereby loosening the plug plant. Then plant it into a larger pot or plant it outside (**SEE** *Planting out*).

POLLINATION GROUPS

When buying fruit trees, it is important to choose the right pollination group. Different varieties flower at varying times, and unless self-fertile each fruit tree needs to be pollinated by a nearby tree that is also in flower. Each type of fruit has its varieties divided into pollination groups depending on when it blossoms – the group number should be supplied on the label. Make sure you choose trees from the same or adjacent groups.

ABOVE Different varieties of fruit trees blossom at different times, so to ensure good pollination choose varieties from compatible pollination groups.

ABOVE By planting in pots you can create soil types that you may not have in your garden: for example, boggy acidic soil is needed for this cranberry plant.

POTS, GROWING IN

Plants grown in pots will need more attention than those in the ground, but do enable those without a garden to grow something of their own. A few simple steps will safeguard your plant's success:

- Always choose the largest pot you can to give each plant as much space as possible to spread its roots and shoots, and to minimize the time you have to spend watering it.
- Check that there is good drainage at the base of the pot, to prevent the roots drowning in soggy compost. Provided it is well-drained, you do not need to add crocks (broken up old pots) or stones or gravel to the bottom of the container. If you can raise the pot off the ground with little pot 'feet' this will also help.

- Use good-quality, multipurpose potting compost (**SEE** *Compost*), and mix in horticultural grit at a ratio of 1:3 for plants that need very good drainage (e.g. rosemary and lavender).
- Water regularly, and check if the pot requires watering daily (or even twice daily for small pots in a hot, sunny spot). **SEE** *Watering*.
- Fertilize the plant regularly through the growing season (from spring to late summer). **SEE** *Fertilizers*.

PRUNING

Pruning is the removal of unwanted branches from a shrub or tree. It is carried out once or twice a year to restrict the size of the plant, to remove dead or damaged wood, and to promote particular growth habits, flowering and fruiting.

ABOVE Prune damaged wood back to a healthy bud.

ABOVE Always cut just above a bud.

All pruning follows the same principles:

- Use sharp, clean secateurs, loppers or a saw, and the appropriate tool for the size of the branch.
- Cut just above a bud; never leave a bud-less stub, as this will die back, look ugly and be more susceptible to disease, which might then spread to the rest of the tree/shrub.
- Remove the 3 Ds before taking out any other branches: the Dead, Diseased and Dying branches. Cut these back to healthy growth.
- Look for the fourth D: Duplicates. Are there two branches growing in the same direction very close to one another? One of them should come out. What about crossing branches? Remove anything that is not within the framework you are after (bearing in mind the points below).
- Look twice, cut once. You cannot stick a branch back on again, so be sure it is the right one to remove.

- Never cut off more than a quarter to a third of the branches at any one time.
- Prune in the dormant season (when the branches are bare) except for cherries and plums (which are pruned in summer).
- Trained fruit trees and shrubs are also pruned in summer to restrict their growth even further.
- **SEE PAGE 171** for sources of more information on pruning.

ROOT BALL
This comprises the roots and the compost/soil that sticks to the roots when the plant is taken out of a pot or the ground.

ROOTSTOCKS
In order to make trees more manageable for gardeners and farmers, fruit trees are actually now two separate plants, grafted together when very young. The grower can

therefore choose not only the variety (the top part) but also the rootstock (which determines the tree's vigour). Some (known as the 'MM' rootstocks) also confer some disease resistance to the whole tree as well.

For most garden situations and trained trees a dwarfing or semi-dwarfing rootstock is preferable, such as 'MM106' for apples, 'Quince C' for pears, 'Pixy' for plums and 'Gisela 5' for cherries. Check the label on the trees you might buy, or talk to the retailer about what varieties are available on which rootstocks before you make your choice (remembering also to think about the *Pollination groups*).

SEASONS

In this book a cool-temperate climate is assumed and so:
- spring is March, April and May;
- summer is June, July and August;
- autumn is September, October and November;
- winter is December, January and February.

Early spring is therefore March, mid-spring April and late spring May and so forth.

If you live in a location with different climatic conditions, some seasonal tasks may fall slightly earlier or later than specified here. Use your neighbours' gardens and vegetable patches as a guide.

SOIL

Most soil types fall somewhere towards the middle of a spectrum, with pure clay at one end and pure sand at the other. It is useful to know roughly what kind of soil you have as it will better inform how you manage your plants.

To assess your soil, take up a handful (add a little water if it is very dry). If you cannot roll it into a ball and it feels gritty, you have predominantly sandy soil. Sandy soils warm up quickly in spring, and are excellent for root crops such as carrots, which can push easily through the soil. They are well-drained, so will not get waterlogged in wet weather, but will also need more watering (and fertilizer, as the nutrients leach out with the water) in dry spells.

Soil that rolls easily into a ball has a proportion of clay in it. If you can form the ball into a sausage, and then loop the sausage into a ring, you have a high clay soil. The sooner in this process it falls apart the less clay there is. Clay soils retain more nutrients, but also more water and so can get soggy. They are harder to cultivate and tend to stick together in big clods. If you do dig over the soil (SEE *Digging*), do so in autumn but leave it in its large clods. The frost will break these down over the winter.

No matter what your soil type, it will be improved by the regular addition of copious quantities of organic matter (SEE *Organic matter*), both dug into the beds and applied as a mulch (SEE *Mulch*). Over time it is possible to get the loveliest, crumbliest, dark brown, nutrient-rich, well-drained soil there is simply by adding organic matter every year or twice a year.

SOWING SEEDS

There are two ways to start a plant from seed: sow and raise it in a seed tray, little pot or modular tray under cover before planting out the little seedling; and sow the seed directly into a large pot or the ground where it will grow all season. Raising young plants in pots/trays requires more equipment, time and space (such as a sunny windowsill, or greenhouse if you have got one) than sowing direct. However it means that you can get earlier harvests (as you can start frost-tender plants indoors long before they would be able to be sown outside), and you put out only successful young plants. Direct sowing can result in patchy rows if some of the seed does not come up, and the seedlings are more at the mercy of the variable weather and pests, but is the only option for some seeds such as root crops like carrots. However and wherever the seeds were sown, once they are in the soil/compost, keep it consistently moist (but not damp), and preferably warm. Germination rates vary between crops – check the seed packet for this and more sowing information. SEE ALSO *Compost, Digging, Plug plants, Successional sowing, Watering.*

SOWING IN A SEED TRAY

Overfill the tray with seed compost, then tap the tray on a surface a couple of times. Using a flat-edged piece of wood in a sawing motion, push off the excess compost from the middle to one side and then from the middle to the other side.

Use the base of another tray to press down the compost surface gently. Water the compost. Put the seeds into your hand and tap the side of your hand as you move it over the compost, to allow the seeds to fall out gradually.

Sprinkle a very thin layer of compost over the top of the seeds. Mark the seed tray with a label, stating the crop, variety and date sown.

SOWING IN A POT OR MODULAR TRAY

Large seeds are best sown in modular trays, which are plastic seed trays divided into a number of cells (the number varies from six large ones to twenty-four or more smaller cells).

Fill the modular tray with compost as for *Sowing in a seed tray* (above) and water. Then push in the seeds, one or two per module. Seeds should always be sown at a depth of twice their size; thus a large bean seed will be sown deeper than a small tomato seed.

Cover the seeds with compost (add a little more if necessary). Mark with a label stating the crop, variety and date sown.

SOWING SEEDS DIRECTLY OUTSIDE

In prepared and weed-free ground, mark your row using a string line (a piece of string tied between small stakes at either end).

Then use a hoe, or the corner of a rake or spade, to scrape out a drill along the line. (A drill is a shallow channel into which a line of seeds are sown.) Water the bottom of the drill.

Sprinkle the seeds thinly along the drill and cover with a little soil. Mark the row with a label stating the crop, variety and date sown.

Alternatively, station sow. This is when the seeds are put in small holes – stations – the required distance apart. Put two or three seeds per station and thin the seedlings to leave the strongest.

BELOW Carrots can be sown successionally.

SOWING, SUCCESSIONAL

With many crops, the harvest can be spread over the season by sowing in small batches over a number of weeks. Rather than sowing at calendar-based intervals, wait until the first seedlings have four leaves before sowing again. Refer to the seed packet for the months you can sow in, and take full advantage of that range.

ABOVE Use a figure-of-eight tie to secure a tomato plant to its cane.

ABOVE Secure a young tree to its stake with a tree tie and cushion. Check and loosen tree ties regularly.

STAKES & SUPPORTS

Climbing beans are best allowed to twine up a wigwam made from bamboo canes or hazel stakes. Tie each young fruit tree and other tall, thin plants to a long and sturdy bamboo cane/hazel stake using a figure-of-eight tie: one loop should go around the stem and the other one around the cane, always tying off against the cane not the plant. Larger trees, while they are establishing (around two years), may need a thicker stake for support. Before you plant the tree hammer this in securely, 5–10cm/2–4in from the trunk, so that the prevailing wind will blow the tree away from the stake. Use a tree tie with a cushion to secure the stake and tree together, and check it every couple of months to see if the tie needs loosening.

Secure bushy plants that need some support, such as chillies, using the three-loop method. Insert a central cane and tie one end of the twine to it. Then mentally divide the plant branches into three sections, and loop twine around each section in turn, returning to loop round the cane between each section. Tie off the twine at the cane. Do this about 15cm/6in above soil level when the plant is 30cm/12in tall, and again if necessary at 30cm/12in above soil level once the plant is 40–50cm/16–20in tall.

THINNING

Sometimes nature is particularly bountiful and provides more than is needed. While it is tempting to leave all the seedlings that germinate, or all the fruit on an apple tree, this will result in a lower-quality harvest, so you need to reduce the number.

Thin the clusters of tiny apples and pears once the plant has already dropped some in late spring; take out the smallest and leave

ABOVE Thin clusters of young apples to allow the remaining fruitlets to develop to a good size.

– depending on the size of the tree – two or three fruit per cluster.

Seedlings sown in modular trays should be thinned so that only one seedling per module remains. Pull out any extra seedlings carefully, leaving the strongest-looking one (not necessarily the tallest).

Crops such as carrots and beetroot that are drill sown will also require excess roots removed to allow the others to develop at the correct spacing. However do not be too hasty in pulling them out. If you wait until all the roots are big enough to be harvested as baby veg, then you can actually use the thinnings (in a root veg tarte Tatin, page 169) rather than having to throw them away, and you will still get a later harvest of bigger vegetables.

SEE ALSO *Sowing seeds*.

TRAINING TREES & SHRUBS

If you think you do not have space for a fruit tree, think again! There are dwarf forms (sometimes called ballerina trees) that can be grown in relatively small pots, as well as trees that can be trained against a wall or fence. The main training forms and the fruits they are suitable for are:

- ballerina trees: a free-standing, particularly small cordon – apples, cherries, pears, plums;
- cordon: a single-stemmed tree trained vertically or diagonally against a wall, fence, trellis or free-standing posts and wires (usually several together) – apples, gooseberries, pears, redcurrants;
- espalier: branches are trained horizontally from the main trunk at intervals – apples, pears;
- fan: branches are trained at angles in a fan shape away from the main trunk – cherries, gooseberries, plums, redcurrants;
- stepover: the main stem is pruned as for a cordon, but it is bent over horizontally about 45cm/18in from the ground to create a low barrier, often used for bed edging – apples, pears.

Training trees and shrubs does take time, and they will also require summer pruning to restrict their growth, but they look very attractive and are surprisingly productive for the space they occupy.

SEE PAGE 171 for sources of information on how to train fruit trees.

WATERING

Watering is one of the basic tasks of gardening, and one that is so often done badly. The main tenets are these:

- Regularly (daily in summer) check if your plants need water by putting your finger into the soil or compost. Many gardening books talk of the ideal soil being 'moist but well-drained'. This apparent

ABOVE Water the bottom of a drill before sowing any seeds.

- Use a rose attachment to the can's spout to slow down and spread the flow, otherwise the soil/compost will get washed away.

WEEDS

There are two types of weed – annual and perennial. Annual weeds germinate fast, grow fast and set seed fast, but are easy to pull out and once they have gone they will not come back, provided they have not had time to set seed. They include plants such as hairy bittercress (*Cardamine hirsuta*), fat-hen (*Chenopodium album*) and groundsel (*Senecio vulgaris*). Perennial weeds live year on year, and all their roots should be removed or they will regrow. Docks (*Rumex*) and some nettles (*Urtica*) belong to this group.

Whether annual or perennial, all weeds are best removed with a hand fork to get all the roots out (or even a spade). If you are short of time you could hoe the beds instead, but any perennial weeds will come back again. Always try and get weeds out before they flower, as weed seeds can persist in the soil for many years: as the adage goes, 'one year's seed . . . seven years' weeds'. But also be aware that, even if you bought in sterile, weed-free topsoil for your garden, you will still get weeds, as the seeds are blown in on the wind or dropped by birds.

Weeding is a task best approached piecemeal. When you go to harvest a crop, pull out a few weeds for five minutes. When you pop out for some fresh air, pull out another five minutes' worth of weeds. This way it never becomes a daunting task that is easy to put off and tough to get through, and the garden stays in good order.

contradiction means that the soil should be not wet or dry but moist. If it feels moist and a few bits stick to your finger it is perfect, come back tomorrow. If it is dry, water! If it is soggy and wet, leave it for a couple of days before checking again.

- When you do water the plants, do so thoroughly, giving the soil a good soak and pots enough that the water is running out of the bottom of the pot (if they are very dry it will do this straight away, so it is better to stand the pot in a bucket of water for a few hours and let it absorb the water that way). Large pots can need several litres of water every day during spells of hot weather.
- Put the spout of the watering can as close as possible to the soil/compost. The water needs to get to the roots, not be splashed over the foliage where the resulting humidity can foster disease.

RIGHT Plants grown indoors, such as this chilli, can be misted with water to aid pollination.

IN THE KITCHEN

If I could give you only one baking tip, it would be that you need to be well prepared. Professional pastry chefs and bakers weigh out all their ingredients in advance, with everything in its own little bowl. I rarely have time to prepare for a bake that thoroughly and anyway that entails a lot of washing up. However it is always wise to make sure you have read the recipe thoroughly, and prepared those items that need a little more input than just weighing out – such as grating the vegetable ingredients – so that you can mix everything and get it in the oven as quickly as possible. All cakes rely on some form of raising agent, whether it is baking powder or the air in whisked eggs, and the longer the batter is standing around the less effective these ingredients will be.

Below I have given some general tips on the techniques used in this book. I have also explained in detail some basic procedures that are common to several recipes, such as how to make pastry.

ALLERGIES & INTOLERANCES
Unfortunately there is often just no substitute for wheat flour or butter in a recipe, and so cakes have long been forbidden fruit to the intolerant or allergic. Although this book does not suggest alternative ingredients, I have included some cakes and other bakes that do not contain gluten, wheat or dairy (SEE PAGE 11). There are also a number of good, gluten-free flour mixes available these days (Doves Farm does an excellent gluten-free baking range). These can be introduced instead of wheat flour without otherwise changing the recipe (you may need a little extra liquid though – try adding a tablespoon or two of milk if needed).

BEATING & WHISKING
To beat a mix, use the paddle attachment on a stand mixer, electric beaters or a wooden spoon. Choose the whisk (attachments) only if the recipe specifically says to whisk.

CHOCOLATE, MELTING
It is always preferable to melt chocolate over a pan of simmering water, as it is easier to control and less likely to burn than if done in a microwave. Break up the chocolate into small pieces of roughly the same size and place in a heatproof (glass or ceramic) bowl that fits snugly over a saucepan of water.

LEFT Prepare everything you need in advance for a stress-free baking experience.
RIGHT Melt chocolate in a bowl set over a saucepan of water, kept simmering on a low heat.

The bottom of the bowl should not touch the water – allow space for it to bubble up too. Put over a medium heat and bring the water to a simmer. Do not stir it (unless you are melting butter with the chocolate) until it has almost all melted. Take the bowl off the saucepan and stir the chocolate until it is smooth and glossy.

CHOCOLATE, SHAVINGS

It is much easier to make chocolate shavings from a large bar than a few small squares. Turn the bar over so the flat side is uppermost. Hold a large knife firmly at both ends, and pull it at an angle across the surface of the chocolate. Thin shavings will roll up in front of the blade. Use the knife to transfer them to the cake – they will melt on your fingers.

CREAM

The recipes here all specify double cream, because it gives a richer, tastier result. However you could use single cream if you wanted, to reduce the calorie count slightly or if it is all you have.

If a recipe needs whipped cream, always use double cream rather than 'whipping cream'. It is smoother and creamier, and whips just as well. Stop a little before you think it is thick enough, because by scraping and spooning it, and especially piping it, you will continue to incorporate air. Whipped cream should be smooth, stiff enough to hold its own weight, but not bitty like the stuff in the whipped cream aerosol cans.

CRUMB LAYER

For a smooth finish to a cake that is iced all over, it is worth doing a crumb layer. Use a little of the buttercream/ganache to spread all over the top and sides of the cake, then leave it to set (put it in the refrigerator briefly if you are short of time). All the crumbs on the cake are now secured in this layer and you can spread over the rest of the buttercream/ganache without them appearing on the finished cake.

DAIRY-FREE

SEE *Allergies & intolerances.*

CRYSTALLIZING FLOWERS

All edible flowers, as well as herb foliage, can be coated in sugar and used as decoration. Crystallizing flowers will also preserve them for a day or so.
　　Begin by pulling the green sepals off the flower (if necessary) and shortening the stem to the desired length.

With a fork, beat a few drops of water into an egg white to loosen it. Using a small (clean!) paintbrush, paint all the surfaces of the flower with egg white, covering both sides of the petals.

Sprinkle liberally with caster sugar on both sides, shake off the excess. Then set on a piece of nonstick baking paper or a plate to dry.

RIGHT Crystallizing primroses (*Primula vulgaris*).

EGGS, WHISKING TO SOFT & STIFF PEAKS

Grease is the enemy of successful egg whisking so always make sure your bowl is as clean as can be – adding a dash of lemon juice to the egg whites helps with this.

Crack each egg and transfer the yolk between the two halves of shell, letting the whites drop into the glass below until you have separated the egg yolk from its whites. Once the yolk and whites have been separated, put the whites into your mixing bowl and the yolk into another bowl. Repeat for all the eggs, always separating each egg one at a time into a glass first, because if a yolk breaks on the last egg of a batch of eggs only that one will be ruined rather than the whole lot. (If the recipe uses both the whites and yolks, great, but if the yolks are spare why not put them towards some crème pâtissière, as for example in the Strawberry tart, see page 148.)

Start whisking the egg whites on a medium–slow setting until they froth up a bit, then turn up to high. It is possible to do this by hand, but a stand mixer or hand-held beaters will save a lot of effort. Keep watching as the egg whites become white and turn opaque; stop whisking frequently to test whether they are ready. They will have reached the soft peaks stage when a small peak of whites droops over at the end when the whisk is removed. They will also not slide around in the bowl when it is tipped: you should also be able to hold the bowl upside-down over your head without the contents falling out!

Stiff peaks are created by the addition of sugar – either in granular or liquid form. Turn the whisk down to the slowest setting and trickle in the sugar gently and slowly. Once it has all been added, turn the whisk back up to high. The egg whites will be ready when they are glossy, firm and the top of a peak does not droop over.

A lot of fuss is made of the risk of over-whisking egg whites so that they lose their structural integrity if they go beyond the stiff peaks stage. However it is a lot easier to under-whisk, which will also result in pancake-flat meringues. The more practised you are at whisking egg whites, the better you will get at knowing when they are at optimum stiffness, but if you are not sure there is absolutely no harm in stopping every 30 seconds to check.

Once whisked, use egg whites as soon as possible.

FOLDING

This technique is generally used for whisked-egg cakes and involves stirring cake batter with the lightest possible touch while combining all the ingredients and keeping as much air in the mixture as possible. Always use a large metal spoon, as it has a thinner edge than a wooden spoon or plastic spatula and will squash fewer air bubbles. Run the spoon round the bottom edge of the bowl and fold the mixture over the top of itself, with an occasional slice through the middle of the bowl as well. It is always worth an occasional scrape across the bottom of the bowl with a spatula though, to gather any unmixed ingredients.

FREEZING

One option to preserve a glut of fruit or vegetables is to freeze them. Although they will lose their fresh texture and some of their juices once defrosted, this is ideal for berries and currants. Put the fresh, washed and dried fruit on a tray in the freezer, ensuring the individual fruits

LEFT Properly whipped egg whites will not fall out of the bowl!

ABOVE Open freeze fruit (here raspberries) on a tray for a day or so, before bagging it up.

are not touching and there are no mouldy ones. Once frozen (after about 24 hours) they can be put into a box or bag for longer-term freezing.

GLUTEN-FREE
SEE *Allergies & intolerances.*

INGREDIENTS
When weighing out ingredients, use the metric or the imperial measures throughout a recipe; never mix the two systems.

Rule number one with ingredients is to buy the best you can afford, and the freshest. Always, always, have your ingredients at room temperature before you start baking. This obviously requires a bit of forward planning, so if you suddenly get the urge to bake and your eggs and butter are in the refrigerator, put the eggs in a glass of warm water and the butter (weighed out first) in the oven for a minute or two as it is warming up. Pastry however requires the butter to be cold.

KNEADING BREAD

To knead with a stand mixer and dough hook, put the appropriate quantity of flour and yeast into the bowl and turn on to the lowest speed. Slowly pour in the wet ingredients and mix for 5 minutes before adding the appropriate quantity of salt and continuing to mix for another 5 minutes.

Alternatively knead by hand. Start by mixing the appropriate quantity of flour, yeast and wet ingredients together in a large bowl until they have come together, then tip out on to a well-floured surface. Bring the dough together in a ball. With one hand on the dough, use your other hand to push it away from you, then fold it back on itself on to the main ball. Turn the ball by 90 degrees and repeat.

Continue kneading for 5 minutes, then spread out the dough into a large disc and sprinkle over the appropriate quantity of salt. Fold the dough back on itself and continue kneading as above for another 5–10 minutes. The dough should feel smooth and elastic.

Once the dough is kneaded, it is ready to prove, in a covered bowl in a warm place, until it has doubled in size.

RIGHT Kneading the dough for the Cranberry couronne (see page 82).

Unless otherwise stated in the recipes in *Grow Your Own Cake*:

- butter is unsalted;
- fruit and vegetables are washed/scrubbed, dried and topped and tailed as necessary;
- eggs are medium-sized;
- milk is semi-skimmed;
- salt is fine, not flaked.

OVEN TEMPERATURES & BAKING TIMES

Oven temperatures are given in degrees Celsius and Fahrenheit for fan ovens, as well as in gas marks.

It is important to know whether the temperature dial on your oven is accurate, so buy an oven thermometer to find out – they are inexpensive and repay themselves tenfold in avoided baking disasters. My own oven is a massive 15°C hotter than the temperature on the dial.

With that in mind, and as the baking time will vary with the tin size and number of tins in the oven, treat the baking time given in this book as a guide rather than a prescription. Do not abandon your cake in the oven and go and do something else, or at least come back a good 10 minutes before the timer will ring.

SEE ALSO *Testing to see if cakes are cooked.*

PASTRY, GLUTEN-FREE

Gluten-free substitutes for plain flour are relatively easy to come by, in mainstream stores as well as specialist health food shops and of course online. To make the pastry recipes gluten-free, replace the plain flour with a gluten-free one (Doves Farm produce a suitable one, **SEE** *Allergies & intolerances*). You may need to add a little more liquid to bring the dough together – use milk or, if dairy is also off-limits, soya or almond milk. Trickle this in a few drops at a time so as not to over-dampen the dough.

PASTRY, TO MAKE

Follow this method when making all the pastries in this book:

Sift the flour, salt and any ground almonds into a large bowl or the bowl of a stand mixer or food processor. Cut the butter into large flat pieces and add them to the flour mix.

Rub in the butter with your fingertips (or use a paddle attachment on the stand mixer or pulse in the food processor) until the butter has evenly coated all the dry mix and it looks like breadcrumbs. Stir in the sugar. Then add the beaten eggs and mix everything (by hand or with the stand mixer/food processor) until it starts to come together as a dough.

Tip out on to a clean, well-floured surface and continue to bring the dough together by hand, kneading it as little as possible, until it has an even consistency.
Shape into a rectangular block, wrap in greaseproof paper and chill in the refrigerator for at least an hour.

PASTRY, TO ROLL OUT & BAKE BLIND

I prefer to make my pastry a little on the wet side, so that the flour that it picks up from the surface does not then make it too dry. You may therefore find the dough a little sticky to start with, but if you keep the surface, rolling pin and your hands well-floured the chilled dough will be easier to work.

Always roll out the pastry as thin as possible, which may mean you have some excess. Return a little to the refrigerator in case you need to patch up a blind-baked pastry case, while the rest is a bonus. Either bake a few extra little pastry cases (fill with fruit and whipped cream – cook's perks), or freeze the dough wrapped in baking paper then sealed in a plastic bag. It will last three months in the freezer (label with the date), by which time you can collect enough scraps to combine them into a whole tart or flan.

Grease the tin/dish with butter. Put loose-bottomed, metal flan tins on to a baking sheet.

Roll out the pastry on a lightly floured surface, lifting and turning it as you go, until it is at the required thinness and/or big enough to line a single tin/dish with some overhang.

For small tarts, cut out discs using the required cutter size. Carefully transfer the pastry to the tin/dish and press gently into the corners and sides. Keep back a small ball of leftover pastry.

Prick the base(s) all over with a fork, line the case(s) with baking paper and fill with baking beans. Any dried beans are fine to use for this, although designated ceramic baking beads will not smell. Rest in the refrigerator for half an hour while preheating the oven to 180°C/350°F/gas mark 4.

Bake for about 20 minutes for a large tart case, 15 minutes for small tarts, checking regularly, until the pastry is dry and light golden brown. Remove the baking paper and beans/beads, and if there are any holes patch them over with the reserved raw pastry. Brush with beaten egg and return to the oven for 10 minutes for a large tart case, 8 minutes for small tarts until dark golden brown. Remove from the oven and once cooled trim the edge of a large tart case with a serrated knife.

PIPING

While it is perfectly possible to bake and decorate all the cakes in this book using only spoons and knives, piping gives a neater finish because you have more control over the process. Proper piping bags make life easier, but any plastic food bag will do. Before spooning the buttercream or meringue into the piping bag, it helps to stand the bag in a tall mug or jug so you have both hands free. There is no need for special nozzles – just cut the end off the bag, to create a hole of the desired width. Twist the bag closed at the top and, if necessary, swing it over your shoulder to move all the mixture down to the point of the bag – *before* you cut the end off!

To create neat, little blobs, such as the Flower meringues (**SEE PAGE 126**), hold the point of the bag just above some baking paper. Squeeze out a little mixture – it will rise up around the bag point – then stop squeezing and push the point down into the blob before pulling it up and out. This should leave a small peak but not a trail of mixture across the paper. If you need to flatten any little peaks, such as on the Blackcurrant mini-pavlovas (**SEE PAGE 132**), use a dampened finger to squash them down gently.

SECURING A CAKE WITH SKEWERS/DOWELS
Two-layer cakes will support themselves, but if you go any higher than that the tiers will need securing to prevent them slipping. Specialist cake dowels are available for this purpose, but wooden skewers or plastic straws do just as good a job. Push each one into the cake before you ice or decorate, making sure you feel each hit the bottom.

Three or four skewers/dowels will be enough, provided they are well-spaced around the cake. Pull the skewers/dowels out of the cake slightly before cutting them so that the tops sit flush with or just below the top of the cake.

TESTING TO SEE IF CAKES ARE COOKED
The first indication that a cake is nearly ready is that a delicious smell will be coming from the oven, but to prevent it sinking make sure it has had at least 75 per cent of its recommended baking time before you open the door (unless it is a Genoese sponge, in which case never open the door before 25 minutes have elapsed). Other signs that a cake is cooked are that it should have risen, the surface should be lightly browned and firm to the touch, and it should have shrunk from the sides of the tin. The best test varies with the type of cake – see the specific recipes – but often it is to insert a wooden skewer into the middle of the cake. Only

ABOVE An uncooked cake will leave wet mixture on the skewer.

ABOVE The skewer will come out clean from a cooked cake.

once the skewer comes out clean is it ready to remove from the oven. Always test each cake tin separately, with a clean skewer.

If for some reason your oven temperature was too high and the cake is not cooked in the middle but browning too fast on top, turn down the temperature to 20°C/50°F/2 gas marks below that stated in the recipe and cover the top of each tin with foil. Check every 5–10 minutes to see if it is ready.

Carefully remove the baking paper from the base of each sponge once it has been turned out of its tin.

TINS

Most people do not have the space to store a huge range of cake tins, and investing in good-quality ones can get expensive. All the bakes in this book therefore use only a small range:

- 2 × deep, round cake tins, 20cm/8in diameter (preferably loose-bottomed with a silicone seal);
- 1 × spring-form, round cake tin, 23–24cm/9–9½in diameter;
- 1 × 12-hole muffin or cupcake tin, with holes about 3cm/1¼in deep;
- 1 × loose-bottomed, metal flan tin, 23–25cm/9–10in diameter;
- 1 × deep pie dish, 25cm/10in diameter;
- 1 × Swiss roll tin, 30 × 20cm/12 × 8in;
- 1 × brownie or shallow roasting tin, 20 × 25 × 3cm/8 × 10 × 1¼in;
- 1–2 × baking sheets or roasting/oven trays;
- 2 × wire cooling racks.

To this list you could also add the optional extras of:

- 1 × set of cookie cutters (although an upturned glass works well as a substitute);
- 2 × deep, round cake tins, 15cm/6in diameter;
- 1 × 12-hole fairy cake tin, with holes about 2cm/¾in deep;
- 1 × mini-sponge tin, with holes of 4–5cm/1½–2in diameter, 12 holes minimum.

ABOVE Most of the recipes in this book use only a small range of bakeware.

When buying bakeware, always get the best you can afford. Plenty are advertised as nonstick, but this is not necessary as I would always grease and line these tins anyway. Loose-bottomed tins are worth the little extra money though. Few will leak batter these days, but a silicone seal will make sure that they do not.

Tin sizes are sadly not standardized. Use tins as close to the recommended size as you can, but do not run out and buy a new pie dish because yours is 23cm/9in diameter rather than 25cm/10in. Just be aware that if the tin is larger, the filling will be shallower within it and the baking time may need to be slightly shorter to compensate.

Cut out the baking paper lining before greasing the tin – remove the base and draw around it to ensure a snug fit. If you are really short of time it is possible to buy pre-cut liners, but they are vastly more

ABOVE A good set of cookie cutters is worth investing in.

expensive. Better, when you are baking, to cut out a few extra discs in case of cake emergencies in the future.

Grease tins with a thin layer of unsalted butter (or oil, if you need to be dairy-free), making sure that you have covered all of the base and sides. Keep old butter wrappers for this purpose. Take care that you do not add too much grease, as this will result in a crunchy, browned edge to your cakes.

TOASTING NUTS

Toasting the nuts is a step that it is very tempting to skip, but I would urge you not to, because the difference in flavour is enormous. Preheat the oven to 180°C/350°F/gas mark 4. Spread the nuts in a single layer on a baking sheet. Use your nose as a guide as to how long to cook them: when

the aromas start to fill the kitchen they are done. Some approximate times are:
- walnuts and pecans – 7–8 minutes;
- hazelnuts – 8–9 minutes.

TROUBLESHOOTING

The most common things to go wrong in baking are the mix curdling or splitting. Fortunately both are easily remedied.

Curdling can occur when eggs are added to creamed butter and sugar, which then turns into a lumpy, watery mess. Usually this is because the eggs are too cold. To remedy the mix, take a couple of tablespoons of pre-weighed flour and add them to the curdled ingredients, then beat thoroughly and quickly. Add more flour until the mix combines into a smooth batter again, then pick up the recipe where you left off.

Chocolate when overheated can split – it will then look oily and behave like flubber. This may occur in recipes such as for brownies and ganaches. Using a shallow, wide bowl when melting the chocolate is a good preventative measure, as is cooling the mixture (for 10–15 minutes in the refrigerator) and beating, but they do not always remedy the problem.

WHEAT-FREE
SEE *Allergies & intolerances.*

SPRING & SUMMER CAKES

GOOSEBERRIES

It is worth the odd thorn in the finger to pick the fuzzy green gooseberries that herald the start of the summer soft fruit season. Along with currants, gooseberries are less easy to find in the shops than other berries.

BEST VARIETIES

'Careless' crops early in the season and is good for cooking, while 'Invicta' provides a reliably good harvest and has some resistance to mildew (a common problem in gooseberries). The red berries of 'Whinham's Industry' are sweet enough to eat raw.

PLANTING

Plants can be bought bare-root in winter or container-grown year-round. They are happy

in a little shade and will also appreciate shelter from winds and a well-drained soil, but the early flowers of gooseberry plants will be killed by the cold, so do not plant in a frost pocket. Gooseberries can be trained against a wall or fence in a fan shape or as a cordon. Alternatively a bush can be raised off the ground on a tall leg to create a standard, under which other plants can be grown. Allow 1.25m/4ft between plants growing as bushes; on a wall or fence allow 30cm/12in between cordons and 1.5m/5ft between fans. Gooseberries will happily grow in large pots too, and in fact this can be preferable because the plants can then be moved under cover (into a greenhouse for example) in late winter to get an earlier harvest than plants growing outside.

MAINTENANCE

Prune bushes to maintain a goblet shape of 8–10 branches. Remove old, dead or diseased branches back to the main stem in early spring and shorten new growth by one-half in midsummer. On cordons shorten all new growth to five buds in summer, then back to one bud in winter. To prune a fan, treat each branch as if it were a cordon. Mulch gooseberries in spring.

HARVEST

Pick half the berries from mid- to late spring, and leave the rest to swell and sweeten until early or midsummer. Keep a small stalk on the berry to avoid tearing the skin. Top and tail in the kitchen later.

LEFT Beware of thorns when harvesting gooseberries.
RIGHT Top and tail gooseberries by nicking the old flower and stem off with a knife.

BAKE

Fresh fruit cake (see page 66)
Gooseberry & elderflower
cake (see page 48)

GOOSEBERRY & ELDERFLOWER CAKE

MAKES A TWO-LAYER CAKE

YOU WILL NEED

2 × deep, round cake tins, 20cm/8in diameter, greased and base-lined

INGREDIENTS

Gooseberry compote:
500g/1lb 2oz gooseberries
100–150g/3½–5oz caster sugar

Elderflower syrup:
75g/2½oz caster sugar
75ml/2½fl oz water
6–7 elderflowers

Cake:
6 eggs
180g/6oz caster sugar
180g/6oz plain flour
90g/3oz unsalted butter, melted
8 tbsp elderflower syrup
Icing sugar, to dust (for decoration)

Cream:
100ml/3½fl oz double cream
4 tbsp elderflower syrup

Things that grow together, go together, as the saying goes. This cake of early summer harvests is perfect for those first tentative picnics of the season.

METHOD

- **For the compote**, put the gooseberries and 100g/3½oz of the sugar in a saucepan with a splash of water and bring to a simmer, stirring to dissolve the sugar. Cook over a medium–low heat until the fruit is soft, then push through a sieve into a bowl. Add more sugar to taste and leave to cool.
- **For the syrup**, follow the flower syrup instructions in Flower meringues (see page 126).
- **For the cake**, preheat the oven to 180°C/350°F/gas mark 4. Whisk the eggs and sugar together (this should be done using a stand mixer or electric beaters for best effect) until a little mix trickled over the surface leaves a trail, and the mixture has at least doubled in volume. Sift in half the flour and fold in. Sift in the rest of the flour and fold in. Finally trickle the melted butter into the batter, folding as you go to minimize the loss of volume, and continue folding until everything is incorporated. Divide between the two tins and bake for 25–30 minutes until golden, and firm to the touch. Do not open the oven door before 25 minutes have elapsed or the cake will sink. Remove from the oven and turn over on to a wire rack, but leave the tins over the top of the sponges for 10 minutes, then remove them. Once cool, drizzle each sponge with 4 tbsp elderflower syrup.
- **For the cream**, whisk the cream and syrup together until stiff enough to spread.

TO ASSEMBLE

Spread the compote and then the cream over one layer of sponge. Place the other sponge carefully on top and dust with icing sugar just before serving.

GROW

Edible flowers (see page 124)
Gooseberries (see page 46)

CARROTS

When I first started growing my own vegetables, I had a friend who thought carrots is carrots is carrots. I presented him with my home-grown roots for dinner, pulled from the soil that afternoon. 'Oh', he said, 'so that's what carrots are supposed to taste like.'

ABOVE Use a hand fork to harvest carrots, to avoid breaking the roots.

BAKE
Carrot & almond cake
(see facing page)
Carrot cake (see page 52)
Carrot cookies (see page 118)
Root veg tarte Tatin
(see page 169)

BEST VARIETIES

For recipes that call for blended or grated carrot, sweet, juicy, long, blunt-ended varieties are best, such as 'Sugarsnax 54', 'St Valery', any of the 'Nantes' type or the shorter 'Amsterdam Forcing' for growing in pots. When using whole carrots, as in Root veg tarte Tatin (see page 169), baby carrot varieties such as 'Paris Market' are a good choice, and also suitable for growing in pots.

PLANTING

Sow carrots in a sunny spot in spring, and again at intervals until late summer. Scatter the seed thinly in a drill in well-prepared soil free from large stones. Small carrots can be grown in pots, and this is actually preferable to growing them in heavy clay soils.

MAINTENANCE

Carrot flies are attracted by the scent of the foliage so avoid brushing it while tending the plants. To protect the crop from such pests, cover with horticultural fleece or fine mesh. Clear plastic tunnels can also be used if aired daily. Check the edges and folds regularly for slugs and snails. Thin the seedlings once the roots have grown to a usable size, leaving one plant every 10cm/4cm or so.

HARVEST

Satisfying as it is to just pull up carrots using the foliage, this should be avoided so the root does not break; instead use a fork to lever them out of the ground. Carrot thinnings provide the first harvest, while the main crop will be ready around four months after sowing.

CARROT & ALMOND CAKE

GF WF DF
WITHOUT FROSTING

MAKES A TWO-LAYER CAKE

YOU WILL NEED
2 × deep, round cake tins, 20cm/8in diameter, greased and base-lined

INGREDIENTS

Cake:
6 eggs
250g/8oz light brown muscovado sugar
450g/1lb peeled and finely grated carrots
1 orange, zest
300g/10oz ground almonds
150g/5oz rice flour
1 tsp baking powder
2 tsp ground cinnamon
1 tsp ground ginger

Frosting:
350g/12oz icing sugar
150g/5oz cream cheese
25g/1oz unsalted butter
½ tsp vanilla extract

Dairy-free water icing:
100g/3½oz icing sugar
water

Dairy-free filling:
100g/3½oz apricot jam

Decoration:
75g/2½oz walnuts and/or pecans, toasted
1 orange, zest

This gluten-free carrot cake is best eaten the day after making, so bake the sponges in advance and assemble the cake at the last minute. For a dairy-free cake, top with the water icing instead of the frosting, and fill with apricot jam.

METHOD

- **For the cake**, preheat the oven to 180°C/350°F/gas mark 4. Whisk the eggs and sugar together until pale, frothy and increased in volume. Fold in the carrots and orange zest. Mix the almonds, rice flour, baking powder and spices together, then sift and fold into the mix. Divide between the two tins and bake for 30–35 minutes, until a skewer comes out clean. Remove from the oven and leave in the tins for 10 minutes. Then turn out on to a wire rack to cool completely.
- **For the frosting**, sift the icing sugar into a bowl, then add the cream cheese, butter and vanilla extract. Beat together for 5–8 minutes until creamy. (If your kitchen is warm, it can help to chill the frosting for half an hour or so in the refrigerator before spreading on the cakes.)
- **For the dairy-free water icing**, sift the icing sugar into a bowl and add water a few drops at a time, stirring until it turns to a smooth paste.

TO ASSEMBLE

Use half the frosting to sandwich the two sponges together, then spread the rest over the top. Decorate with the toasted nuts and orange zest.

For a dairy-free cake, sandwich the two sponges together with the jam. Spread the water icing over the top and decorate with the toasted nuts and orange zest.

GROW
Carrots (see facing page)

CARROT CAKE

MAKES A TWO-LAYER CAKE

YOU WILL NEED

2 × deep, round cake tins, 20cm/8in diameter, greased and base-lined

INGREDIENTS

Cake:
200g/7oz peeled carrots
2 tbsp natural yogurt
1 tbsp orange juice
330g/11oz plain flour
300g/10oz light brown muscovado sugar
2 tsp ground cinnamon
1 tsp ground ginger
1½ tbsp baking powder
180g/6oz unsalted butter
3 eggs

Candied carrot:
1 peeled carrot
70g/2½oz caster sugar
70ml/2½fl oz water

Buttercream:
300g/10oz icing sugar
150g/5oz unsalted butter
3 tsp lemon juice, to taste

Decoration:
1 lemon, zest
75g/2½oz walnuts and/or pecans, toasted

Perhaps the most well-known of all the vegetable cakes, and with good reason, carrot cake comes in many guises. This sponge version is lightly spiced, moist and includes a zesty buttercream. It is light enough for baking with fresh, sweet carrots in summer. For more of a winter-warmer, try the Parsnip winter cake (see page 95).

METHOD

- **For the cake**, preheat the oven to 170°C/325°F/gas mark 3. Grate the carrots, then blitz in a food processor or blender with the yogurt and orange juice to form a rough purée. Set aside. Sift the flour, sugar, spices and baking powder into a large bowl, then beat in the butter until it has coated the dry ingredients and the mix looks like breadcrumbs. Beat in the eggs until just incorporated, and then the carrot purée for 2–3 minutes. Divide between the two tins. Bake for 30 minutes, or until a skewer comes out clean. Then remove from the oven and turn out the cakes to cool on a wire rack.
- **For the candied carrot**, using a zester or small knife, pare long, thin strips of carrot into a small saucepan. Then add the sugar and water. Bring to a simmer over a medium heat and cook for about 5 minutes, until a thin syrup has formed. Hook out the carrot strips and leave to cool on a wire rack.
- **For the buttercream**, sift the icing sugar and beat with the butter to combine, then add lemon juice to taste. Beat for 5–10 minutes until light and fluffy.

TO ASSEMBLE

Use half the buttercream to sandwich the two layers of cake together, and the other half to cover the top. Grate over the lemon zest and finish by sprinkling over the toasted nuts and candied carrot.

GROW

Carrots (see page 50)
Lemons (see page 119)

RHUBARB

Rhubarb comes back year on year, and needs minimal maintenance. Its pink stems are a welcome sight in early spring – the first bounty of the new season.

BEST VARIETIES

'Timperley Early' and 'Hawke's Champagne' both give early, sweet harvests (the clue is in the name). 'Victoria' is a reliable, later-season cropper.

PLANTING

Rhubarb will happily grow in a bit of shade or full sun, and is perfect to stick in that spot you do not know what else to do with. A rich soil is better than a sandy one, but an annual mulch will help out plants in any soil – take care not to cover the plant's crown though, or it may rot. Plant dormant crowns in autumn or winter, and allow a square metre/yard for each plant. Rhubarb is not an ideal candidate for a pot, but it could be grown in a very large one.

MAINTENANCE

Pull off any stems/leaves that die back in summer, and clear all the old leaves away in autumn, to expose the plant to the cold (it needs this to grow well the following year). Should a flower spike appear, cut it off at the base.

To get rhubarb's neon-pink, tender stems early in the season, you need to force the plant by putting a pot, bucket or bin over the top of the plant in mid-winter. The container needs to be tall enough for the stems to grow up underneath, and it must exclude all light. A dustbin, weighted down on top, is not attractive but effective; traditional clay forcing pots are prettier but expensive. If you want to force your rhubarb, have three or more plants and force one a year in rotation to give them time to recuperate because forcing takes a lot of energy out of the plant. Similarly wait at least a year before forcing a new plant.

RIGHT Pull, rather than cut, rhubarb stems from the crown.

HARVEST

Forced stems are ready to pick in early spring, unforced 3–4 weeks later. Gather only the forced stems from a forced plant, and then leave it to recover for the rest of the year. Harvest by pulling the stem away from the plant – if it detaches it is ready. Rhubarb leaves are toxic and should be discarded. Do not pick the stems from a plant in its first year – it needs time to establish.

BAKE
A muffin for all seasons
(see page 92)
Rhubarb crumble &
custard cake (see page 56)

ABOVE Terracotta jars can be used to force rhubarb for an early crop.

GROW
Rhubarb (see page 54)

RHUBARB CRUMBLE & CUSTARD CAKE

SERVES 8–10

YOU WILL NEED

2 × deep, round cake tins, 20cm/8in diameter, greased and base-lined

INGREDIENTS

Crumble topping:

40g/1½oz plain flour
40g/1½oz porridge oats
40g/1½oz unsalted butter
40g/1½oz light brown muscovado sugar

Cake:

600g/1lb 5oz rhubarb, trimmed and cut into 0.5cm/¼in pieces
350g/12oz plain flour
1 tbsp baking powder
100g/3½oz ground almonds
1 tsp ground ginger
250g/8oz unsalted butter
150g/5oz caster sugar
4 eggs
¼ tsp vanilla extract

Buttercream:

350g/12oz icing sugar
50g/2oz custard powder
150g/5oz unsalted butter
50ml/2fl oz double cream

Rhubarb crumble is one of those puddings I always think will be a good idea, then find it is a bit overwhelming. This cake brings together rhubarb, a crumble topping and some custard (in the buttercream) without being overpowering.

METHOD

- **For the crumble topping**, mix the flour and oats together, then rub in the butter. It is fine to leave some small chunks of butter. Stir in the sugar and set aside.
- **For the cake**, preheat the oven to 170°C/325°F/gas mark 3. Toss the rhubarb pieces in 3 tbsp of the flour. Mix the remaining flour with the baking powder, ground almonds and ginger and set aside. Cream the butter and sugar together, then beat in the eggs, one by one, and the vanilla extract. Stir in the flour mix until everything is incorporated. Stir in the rhubarb. Divide the mixture between the two tins and spread as level as you can (it is quite a sticky, lumpy batter). Scatter the crumble topping in an even layer over the top of the mixture in one tin. Bake for 50–60 minutes until a skewer comes out clean. Leave in the tins for 10 minutes, then turn out on to a wire rack, to finish cooling.
- **For the buttercream**, sift the icing sugar and custard powder into a large bowl. Add the butter and cream and beat (on a slow setting at first for a stand mixer, then a high one) for 5–10 minutes until fluffy.

TO ASSEMBLE

Spread the buttercream over the non-crumble topped sponge, and place the crumbled sponge on it.

BEETROOT

I cannot abide the vacuum-packed or pickled beetroot available in the shops, but home-grown roots are a different story, especially when they are baked in a cake! Beetroot is one of the most reliable vegetables to grow from seed, and the young leaves (eat raw, in salads) are a bonus crop.

BAKE

Beetroot brownies
(see page 108)
Beetroot cake (see page 60)

BEST VARIETIES

'Boltardy' is probably the most widely available and reliable variety, and produces the classic red colour; sweeter, less earthy choices include 'Detroit Dark Red' and 'Sanguina'.

PLANTING

Sow seeds in early spring, and at intervals until early summer, direct into a drill or pot in an open, sunny site. Thin once the baby beets have reached an edible size and leave the rest to grow a little bigger. Aim for 5–10cm/2–4in between each plant. Rows should be 20cm/8in apart.

MAINTENANCE

Weed and water as necessary. Keep an eye out for slugs and snails.

HARVEST

Use the thinnings first, but do not let the remaining roots get too big, as they lose both sweetness and tenderness the larger they grow. Harvest when the beets are bigger than a golf ball but smaller than a tennis ball.

LEFT Thin beetroot once they get to a usable size.

BEETROOT CAKE

MAKES A SINGLE-LAYER CAKE

YOU WILL NEED

1 × spring-form, round cake tin, 23cm/9in
diameter, greased and base-lined

INGREDIENTS

Cake:

4 eggs, separated
250g/8oz dark brown muscovado sugar
400g/14oz peeled and coarsely grated beetroot
200ml/7fl oz vegetable oil or sunflower oil
1 tsp vanilla extract
1 orange, zest
300g/10oz plain flour
3 tsp baking powder
¼ tsp bicarbonate of soda
1 tsp ground cinnamon

Icing:

50g/2oz icing sugar
1 orange, juice

METHOD

- **For the cake**, preheat the oven to
170°C/325°F/gas mark 3. Whisk the egg yolks
and sugar until pale and smooth. Stir in the
beetroot, oil, vanilla extract and orange zest.
Whisk the egg whites to soft peaks and set
aside briefly while you sift the flour, baking
powder, bicarbonate of soda and cinnamon
into the batter and fold them in. Finally
fold in the whisked egg whites. Pour into
the prepared tin and smooth level. Bake for
45–50 minutes until a skewer comes out
clean. Remove from the oven and leave in
the tin for 10 minutes. Then turn out on to
a wire rack to cool completely.
- **For the icing**, sift the sugar into a bowl,
and add the orange juice a little at a time
(you will only need about a quarter of it),
mixing until you have a smooth paste.

TO SERVE

Drizzle with the icing.

Pairing beetroot with the robust
flavourings of orange and cinnamon
creates a moist and deliciously warming
cake, perfect for a rainy afternoon.

GROW

Beetroot (see page 58)

COURGETTES

Once they get going, courgette plants, which are a type of summer squash, will provide you plenty of fruit for cakes, large edible flowers and some more besides.

BAKE
Courgette cake
(see page 62)

BEST VARIETIES

The cylindrical courgettes are easiest to grate, and can be harvested small enough not to be watery. Plants with a bushy, rather than a trailing, habit are easier to manage. Flavoursome varieties include: 'Romanesco', which has the added attraction of large flowers; and yellow-skinned 'Parador'. 'Defender' is reliable, disease-resistant and prolific.

PLANTING

Courgettes need a sunny spot, plenty of space (set bush varieties 90cm/36in apart) and copious amounts of water. Sow in modular trays or small pots under cover in spring, and plant out in early summer after the last frost. Hollow out a slight dip in the soil (about 50cm/20in circumference) and plant in the middle of that, to keep water from running off. You could buy young plants, but you will have a greater choice of variety if you grow from seed.

MAINTENANCE

Water regularly, and check for slugs and snails, which can leave grazing trails across the skins of the courgettes. Plants in large pots should be kept particularly well-watered to minimize the risk of mildew.

HARVEST

For the best flavour harvest courgettes before they get more than 10cm/4in long, using a knife to cut them off at the base. If left on the plant they will quickly turn to marrows, so check as often as possible for new pickings. Pick the male flowers for eating – those without a baby courgette at their base – to ensure you still get the courgettes as well.

BELOW For optimum flavour, harvest courgettes when they are still small.

COURGETTE CAKE

MAKES A SINGLE-LAYER CAKE

YOU WILL NEED

1 × spring-form, round cake tin, 23cm/9in diameter, greased and base-lined

INGREDIENTS

Cake:
180g/6oz unsalted butter
250g/8oz caster sugar
2 eggs
400g/14oz baby courgettes, finely grated
2 lemons, zest
350g/12oz plain flour
1½ tbsp baking powder

Icing:
100g/3½oz icing sugar
250g/8oz mascarpone cheese

Decoration:
1 lemon, zest
1 lime, zest

Small, flavourful courgettes make a great cake ingredient, contributing flavour, moisture and an attractive summery green speckling to a sponge.

METHOD

- **For the cake**, preheat the oven to 160°C/325°F/gas mark 3. Beat the butter and sugar together until light and fluffy, then add the eggs one at a time, beating well to incorporate after each one. Stir in the courgettes and lemon zest, then sift in the flour and baking powder. Fold everything together quickly but carefully. Pour into the tin and spread level. Bake for 45 minutes, until a skewer comes out clean. Remove from the oven and leave for 10 minutes in the tin. Then turn out on to a wire rack to cool completely.
- **For the icing**, sift the icing sugar into a large bowl and add the mascarpone. Beat together with a fork until smooth.

TO ASSEMBLE

Spread the icing over the sponge and scatter with the lemon and lime zest.

GROW

Courgettes (see page 61)
Lemons (see page 119)

RASPBERRIES

If you have access to a range of varieties you can be picking enough fruit for using all summer (and autumn) long.

BEST VARIETIES

There are two distinct groups of raspberries: summer and autumn fruiting. The summer group is then divided into early, mid-season and late fruiting varieties. Of the summer varieties, 'Joan J'

is a good choice for mid- to late crops and 'Glen Cova' for an early summer harvest. 'Autumn Bliss' is a reliable and widely available autumn fruiter.

PLANTING

Raspberries are sold as bare-root or potted canes. Plant in spring, in a well-drained soil. They will happily grow in some shade as well as full sun, and so will do well against a wall or fence. Tie their long canes into horizontal wires either fixed between two posts or to a wall/fence. Two wires – one at 60cm/24in above the ground, another 60cm/24in above that – will be sufficient; bend over any growth higher than the top wire and tie in again. Alternatively plant raspberries around a wigwam, and tie into that, or against an archway. It is possible to grow raspberries in a large pot, tied to a central post or wigwam. New varieties more suitable for pot cultivation are now being introduced.

MAINTENANCE

Mulch the canes well in spring, and make sure they are well-watered in dry spells, especially once they are flowering and fruiting. Pruning is straightforward: remove the canes that have fruited, as they will not produce more fruit. Autumn-fruiting varieties bear fruit on canes that developed earlier in the season, so the whole lot can be cut to the ground in winter/ early spring. Summer-fruiting raspberries bear fruit on canes produced the previous summer, so always have both fruiting and new canes. In autumn cut down the old summer-fruiting canes, and tie in the greener new canes.

HARVEST

Pick every couple of days – raspberries are ripe when they pull away easily from their central plugs.

BAKE

A muffin for all seasons (see page 92)
Chocolate & raspberry bean cake
(see page 68)
Fresh fruit cake (see page 66)
Fruity pizza (see page 142)
Raspberry & white chocolate roll
(see page 88)
Shades of berry cake
(see page 76)

ABOVE Some raspberries will be easy to spot but check carefully under the leaves for ripe raspberries lurking beneath.

BORLOTTI BEANS

Beans such as adzuki and kidney are widely used in baking but cannot be grown successfully in cool-temperate climates. Borlotti beans make a great alternative and, with their red-and-cream-speckled pods, are a very attractive addition to the veg patch.

BEST VARIETIES

'Lingua di Fuoco 2' is the best climbing variety of borlotti bean, but if you do not have the option of growing up a wigwam or trellis try the dwarf type 'Splendido'.

PLANTING

A sunny site is needed for good bean development and soil rich in organic matter so dig in plenty of compost the previous autumn and add some more to the planting holes. Borlotti beans are frost tender, so either sow under cover in spring and plant out in early summer after the last frost, or sow direct into the ground in early summer. These beans can be grown in large pots, but climbing varieties will still need a wigwam of hazel stakes or canes to grow up.

MAINTENANCE

Encourage climbing beans to twine around the wigwam supports, and stake dwarf beans, using the three-loop system (see page 26), to avoid the weight of the pods pulling the plants over. Keep plants well-watered, especially in dry periods, to ensure the beans develop well and the plants do not succumb to diseases such as mildew.

HARVEST

The beans will be ready to harvest in late summer or early autumn, when the pods are fat with the beans inside. Pick and use the podded beans straight away, or dry them to store and use later. If you are storing the beans, leave the pods on the plant to dry first, but pick them before any prolonged wet weather is forecast or they begin to split and drop the beans.

Then remove their pods and leave the Borlotti beans in a warm, dry place until completely desiccated. Store in an airtight container.

BAKE
Chocolate & raspberry bean cake (see page 68)

ABOVE Beans will twine themselves around a wigwam of canes and do not need tying in.

FRESH FRUIT CAKE

MAKES A TWO-LAYER CAKE (OR FOUR LAYERS/TWO TIERS)

YOU WILL NEED

Two-layer sponge:

2 × deep, round cake tins, 20cm/8in diameter, greased and base-lined

Four-layer/two-tier sponge:

2 × deep, round cake tins, 20cm/8in diameter, greased and base-lined

2 × deep, round cake tins, 15cm/6in diameter, greased and base-lined

3–4 × wooden skewers or dowels

INGREDIENTS

For two layers	(For four layers)
Cake:	
300g/10oz plain flour	(450g/15oz)
4 tsp baking powder	(2 tbsp)
155g/5½oz unsalted butter	(230g/8oz)
250g/8oz caster sugar	(375g/12oz)
3 medium eggs	(4 large eggs)
100ml/3½fl oz milk	(150ml/5fl oz)
1 tsp vanilla extract	(1½ tsp)
150g/5oz fresh berries/currants such as raspberries, blueberries and/or currants	(225g/7½oz)
Filling and topping:	
400ml/¾ pint double cream, whipped	(600ml/1 pint)
500g fresh fruit such as raspberries, blueberries, strawberries, currants and/or cherries	(750g)
edible flowers (optional), for decoration	

This is a bucolic summer feast of a cake, a spectacular but simple bake. Light vanilla sponges full of fresh fruit are sandwiched with cream and loaded with as much fruit as they will take. Use whatever fruit you have in abundance.

METHOD

- Preheat the oven to 180°C/350°F/gas mark 4. Set aside 3 tbsp (4 tbsp) of the flour, then sift the remaining flour and the baking powder into a large bowl and mix well. Add the butter and beat using the paddle attachment on a stand mixer (or rub in by hand) until the mix resembles breadcrumbs and all the flour is coated. Stir in the sugar.
- Briefly beat the eggs and vanilla extract into the milk with a fork, then pour into the mix. Beat to incorporate, if possible using a high setting, for 2 minutes.
- Divide between the tins. Toss the fruit in the reserved flour and scatter evenly over the top of the batter.
- Bake for 25 minutes (25–30 minutes, the small tins may need to come out before the larger). Remove from the oven and leave in the tins for 10 minutes. Then turn out on to a wire rack to cool completely.

TO ASSEMBLE

Two-layer sponge:

- Spread one-third of the whipped cream over one sponge and scatter with one-third of the fruit. Lay the other sponge on top, spread over the remaining the cream and top with the remaining fruit and edible flowers, if using.

Four-layer/two-tier sponge:

- Spread one-third of the whipped cream over one of the larger sponges and scatter with one-third of the fruit. Lay the other sponge on top and spread with half of the remaining cream. Place a small sponge (off-centre works best) on top, and cover the top of that with half of the remaining cream and one-quarter of the remaining fruit. Set the final sponge on the top and secure the whole cake with wooden skewers or dowels. Spread the top with the remaining cream and use the remaining fruit to cover the top of that and the bottom tier. Scatter with edible flowers, if using.

GROW
Berries (see pages 64, 74 and 106)
Cherries (see page 102)
Currants (see pages 122 and 130)
Edible flowers (see page 124)

CHOCOLATE & RASPBERRY BEAN CAKE

MAKES A TWO-LAYER CAKE

YOU WILL NEED

2 × deep, round cake tins,
20cm/8in diameter, greased and
base-lined

INGREDIENTS

Beans:
200g/7oz dried or 400g/14oz
fresh borlotti beans

Cake:
6 eggs, separated
200ml/7fl oz sunflower oil
1 tbsp vanilla extract
¼ tsp salt
200g/7oz plain dark
    chocolate, melted
    (70 per cent cocoa solids)
250g/8oz light brown
    muscovado sugar
50g/2oz cocoa powder

Filling and topping:
100g/3½oz raspberry jam
100g/3½oz plain dark
    chocolate, melted
    (70 per cent cocoa solids)
100g/3½oz fresh raspberries

This is one of those dark, rich, fudgy chocolate cakes for the days when ordinary cake just will not do. Using beans for the substance of the cake means it is gluten- and dairy-free (provided your chocolate contains no milk products). It can also be baked out of season, by using dried beans and omitting the fresh fruit decoration. Substitute blackcurrants or strawberries (and their respective jams) if you prefer.

METHOD

- **For the beans**, soak dried beans overnight in plenty of cold water. Drain, rinse and put in a saucepan with more cold water. Bring to the boil and boil for half an hour until soft. Bring fresh beans to the boil in cold water and cook until soft. Drain and cool, then weigh out 400g/14oz.
- **For the cake**, preheat the oven to 180°C/350°F/gas mark 4. Put the beans, egg yolks, oil, vanilla extract, salt and melted chocolate into a food processor (or you could use a stick blender) and blend to a thick paste. Pour the chocolate bean mix into a large bowl and set aside while you whisk the egg whites to soft peaks. Add the sugar, cocoa powder and a spoonful of the egg whites to the chocolate bean mix and stir until everything is incorporated, then fold in the rest of the egg whites. Divide between the two tins and bake for 20–25 minutes until there is no wobble in the cake when the tin is shaken and the surface of the cake is slightly cracked. Remove from the oven and leave in the tins for 10 minutes, then turn out each sponge on to a wire rack to cool completely.

TO ASSEMBLE

Sandwich the two layers of cake together with the jam. Pour the melted chocolate over the cake, spreading it so the top is entirely covered and it drips down the sides in places. Finish with the fresh fruit.

GROW

Borlotti beans (see page 65)
Raspberries (see page 64)

FLORENCE FENNEL

Not, perhaps, the most obvious vegetable to bake with, but Florence fennel's aniseed flavour lends itself well to cakes. This bulbous vegetable has a reputation for being difficult to grow, which is largely due to its tendency to bolt in unfavourable weather, but it is worth the little extra time watering so that you can enjoy its crisp bulbs and pretty feathery foliage.

BAKE
Fennel cake
(see page 70)

BEST VARIETIES

'Romanesco' and 'Finale' are both bolt-resistant, and 'Victorio' is good for sowing later in summer.

PLANTING

A little shade and rich, moisture-retentive soil will help prevent Florence fennel bolting in hot weather. Sow direct, in early spring or mid- to late summer. Florence fennel is prone to bolting, so the later sowings will do better, and successional sowing will ensure a harvest even if one batch does bolt. It is also possible to sow in modular trays for planting out once the seedlings have four leaves, but take care not to disturb the roots. Leave 30cm/12in between rows and plants. Florence fennel can also be grown in pots.

MAINTENANCE

Keep the soil around the plants moist, as again this will help minimize bolting, and keep the area free of weeds.

HARVEST

Bulbs will be ready to harvest about three months after sowing. Either pull out the whole bulb, or cut it off, leaving a small stump, which should re-sprout a few smaller leaves.

RIGHT Harvest Florence fennel by pulling up the plant, or cutting it off at the base.

GROW
Florence fennel
(see page 69)

FENNEL CAKE

MAKES A TWO-LAYER CAKE

YOU WILL NEED

2 × deep, round cake tins, 20cm/8in diameter, greased and base-lined

INGREDIENTS

Cake:
600g/1lb 5oz finely chopped Florence fennel, fronds, base and core removed
350g/12oz plain flour
100g/3½oz ground almonds
1 tbsp baking powder
250g/8oz unsalted butter
150g/5oz caster sugar
4 eggs

Ganache glaze:
300ml/½ pint double cream
2 star anise
250g/8oz plain dark chocolate, finely chopped (70 per cent cocoa solids)
50g/1½oz unsalted butter

Decoration:
fennel fronds

Reserve the fronds from your bulb fennel to decorate the top of the cake (put them in a vase of water to keep them fresh). The bright green is set off beautifully by the plain dark chocolate.

METHOD

- **For the cake**, preheat the oven to 160°C/325°F/gas mark 3. Scatter 2 tbsp of the flour over the fennel flesh and toss to coat. Mix the remaining flour, the almonds and baking powder together and set aside. Beat the butter and sugar together until light and fluffy, then incorporate the eggs, one by one, beating well after each addition. Stir in the coated fennel then fold in the flour mix until everything is included. Divide between the two tins and bake for 40–45 minutes until a skewer comes out clean and the fennel is soft. Remove from the oven and leave to cool in the tins for 10 minutes, then turn out on to a wire rack to cool completely.
- **For the ganache glaze**, bring the cream and anise to the boil in a saucepan over a medium heat, then set aside to cool completely. Meanwhile put the chocolate into a large bowl. Bring the cream mix back to just under the boil, then pour half of it through a sieve into the chocolate. Stir until the chocolate is melting, then add the remaining cream mix (again, through a sieve) and the butter, and stir until smooth and glossy.

TO ASSEMBLE

Spread one sponge with a layer of ganache. Set the other sponge on top and use the remaining ganache to coat the top and sides (a crumb layer is useful for a smooth finish). Decorate with the reserved fennel fronds.

GROW

Lemon thyme (see page 111)
Roses (see page 125)

ROSE CAKE

MAKES A TWO-LAYER CAKE

YOU WILL NEED

2 × deep, round cake tins, 20cm/8in diameter, greased and base-lined

INGREDIENTS

Rose syrup:
150g/5oz caster sugar
150ml/5fl oz water
10 rose flowers

Cake:
6 eggs
180g/6oz caster sugar
180g/6oz plain flour
90g/3oz unsalted butter, melted
4 tbsp rose syrup

Buttercream:
360g/13oz icing sugar
100g/3½oz unsalted butter
7 tbsp rose syrup
Red/pink food colouring (optional)

Decoration:
Rose flowers or petals
Sprigs of foliage (e.g. lemon thyme)

When eating this pretty cake you may have the sensation of walking through a rose garden: a tantalizing scent and flavour of rose that is distinct but not overpowering.

METHOD

- **For the syrup**, follow the flower syrup instructions for flower meringues (see page 126).
- **For the cake**, preheat the oven to 180°C/350°F/gas mark 4. Whisk the eggs and sugar together (for best effect use a stand mixer or electric beaters) until a little mix trickled over the surface leaves a trail, and the mixture has doubled or tripled in volume. Sift in half the flour and fold in. Sift in the remaining flour and fold in. Finally trickle the butter into the batter, folding as you go to minimize the loss of volume, and continue folding until everything is incorporated. Divide between the two tins and bake for 25–30 minutes until golden, firm and springy to the touch. Do not open the oven door before 25 minutes have elapsed or the cake will sink. Remove from the oven and turn over on to a wire rack but leave the tins over the top of the sponges for 10 minutes, then remove the tins. Once cool, drizzle each sponge with 2 tbsp of rose syrup.
- **For the buttercream**, sift the icing sugar into a bowl and add the butter. Beat until combined, then, still beating on slow speed, trickle in the rose syrup and a few drops of food colouring. Beat at high speed for 5–10 minutes until light and fluffy.

TO ASSEMBLE

Use one-third of the buttercream to sandwich the two sponges together. Spread the remaining buttercream over the top and sides. Arrange rose flowers or petals on the top and stick the foliage sprigs around the edge.

BLUEBERRIES

It is strange that it took until relatively recently for this North American plant to spread to fruit cages and farms elsewhere in the world. Blueberries are not difficult to grow, are suitable for most climates and have pretty blossom and stunning autumn leaf colour as well as delicious fruit.

BAKE
A muffin for all seasons
(see page 92)
Fresh fruit cake (see page 66)
Shades of berry cake
(see page 76)

BEST VARIETIES

Large-sized berries are not necessarily the best for baking, as their higher water content means less intense flavour and soggy cakes. Therefore choose varieties such as 'Rubel' and 'Herbert'. You will get more berries on each plant if you have more than one bush, because pollination will improve, but you will still get some harvest from one plant.

PLANTING

Blueberries like a sunny spot in well-drained, acidic soil, but if your patch does not have such soil conditions you can grow them in a large pot using ericaceous compost mixed with some composted bark. They will grow, but not fruit as well, in some shade. In autumn or spring buy container-grown plants to put in the ground or a pot. Space plants 1.5m/5ft apart.

MAINTENANCE

Keep plants in moist soil, especially in pots in hot weather. Use rainwater if possible, not just for the environmental reasons, but because tap water tends to be alkaline and will affect the soil's acidity levels. Mulch in spring with composted bark or pine needles, or ericaceous compost. As with all soft fruit, the berries will be a target for birds, so you may need to net the plants as the fruit ripens. Very little pruning is needed. Once the plant has reached full size (once it is 4–5 years old), remove any dead or diseased branches, and a few of the oldest branches, to thin out the growth.

HARVEST

Blueberries are ready to pick when they are soft, completely blue and have developed that characteristic silver bloom on their skin.

LEFT For maximum sweetness in the blueberries, bake them as soon as possible after harvesting.
RIGHT Harvest blueberries when they are dark blue and juicy.

GROW

Blackcurrants (see page 130)
Blueberries (see page 74)
Raspberries (see page 64)
Strawberries (see page 106)

SHADES OF BERRY CAKE

MAKES A FOUR-LAYER CAKE

YOU WILL NEED

- 1 × deep, round cake tin, 20cm/8in diameter, greased and base-lined (used four times)
- 3–4 × wooden skewers or dowels

INGREDIENTS

Cake, per layer:
- 200g/7oz plain flour
- 2½ tsp baking powder
- ½ tsp bicarbonate of soda
- small pinch of salt
- 100g/3½oz unsalted butter
- 150g/5oz caster sugar
- 2 eggs
- 140g/4½oz puréed blackcurrants or raspberries or blueberries or strawberries

Frosting for four layers (two layers in brackets):
- 200g/7oz caster sugar (100g/4oz)
- 80ml/2½fl oz golden syrup (40ml/1½fl oz)
- 5 tbsp water (2½ tbsp)
- 4 egg whites (2 egg whites)

Decoration:
- 250g/8oz blueberries

Having four layers, each one flavoured with a different berry (OK, so blackcurrants are not berries, but I could not resist the title), this cake is undeniably large. However quantities are given per layer, so you can scale it down if you want; halve the frosting quantities for a two-layer cake. The fruit is blitzed then mixed into the cake batter, so it is a good choice for berries that do not look good enough to be on display.

METHOD

- **For the cake**, make each tier individually. Preheat the oven to 180°C/350°F/gas mark 4. Sift the flour, baking powder, bicarbonate of soda and salt into a large bowl and mix together. Add the butter and beat until the mix resembles breadcrumbs and the butter is evenly coating the flour. Stir in the sugar. Beat the eggs briefly into the fruit purée and then add it all to the dry mix. Mix until incorporated, then beat for a further 2 minutes (turn the stand mixer to high if you are using one). Pour into the tin and bake for 30 minutes until a skewer comes out clean. Remove from the oven and leave in the tin for 10 minutes, then turn out on to a wire rack to cool completely. Repeat for the other one or three layers, as appropriate, using different fruit.
- **For the frosting**, put the sugar, syrup and water in a saucepan over a low heat and stir until the sugar is dissolved. Start whisking the egg whites as you bring the syrup to the boil. Once the egg whites have reached soft peaks and the syrup is boiling, turn the whisk to slow and trickle the syrup into the egg whites, whisking all the time. Turn up to a medium speed again, and whisk for up to 10 minutes until cool, glossy and firm.

TO ASSEMBLE

Lay the blackcurrant sponge on a plate and spread with a fairly thin tier of frosting. Set the raspberry sponge on top, and spread with frosting, then the blueberry sponge, more frosting, finally finishing with the strawberry sponge. Push the skewers or dowels vertically through all the tiers to prevent any slipping. Spread a thin layer of frosting over the top and sides as a crumb layer, then put the cake in the refrigerator for half an hour, before taking out and spreading the remaining frosting over the top and sides. Cover the entire of the top of the cake with the blueberries.

AUTUMN & WINTER CAKES

CRANBERRIES

Cranberries are ideal plants for container growing: they need acidic, boggy soil, which is more easily supplied in a pot than by constructing a special bed (unless of course your garden soil is naturally boggy and acidic). Provided they have these conditions, cranberries are low-maintenance crops, and the leaves produce good autumn colour too. They have a low-growing, spreading habit.

BEST VARIETIES

'Early Black' bears its berries in late summer, while 'McFarlin' has large cranberries.

PLANTING

Buy cranberries in containers for planting at any time of year. Repot into large (at least 30cm/12in diameter) pots with some, but not necessarily good, drainage, using ericaceous compost. Plants will tolerate some shade.

MAINTENANCE

Keep the soil consistently moist, if possible using rainwater rather than tap water, as the pH of tap water will reduce the soil/compost's acidity. In early spring, prune out any dead or diseased branches and thin stems where growth has become overcrowded.

HARVEST

Pick the fruits in autumn, once they have coloured to a deep red. They will keep well in the refrigerator, and even better in the freezer.

BAKE
Cranberry couronne
(see page 82)

LEFT Scarlet cranberries brighten the autumn garden and the winter table.

CRANBERRY COURONNE

MAKES ONE LOAF OF BREAD

YOU WILL NEED

1 × baking sheet, lined with baking paper

INGREDIENTS

Cranberry sauce:
150g/5oz cranberries, fresh or frozen
2 tsp water
60g/2oz caster or granulated sugar

Bread:
60g/2oz unsalted butter
250ml/9fl oz milk
500g/1lb 2oz strong white bread flour
1½ tsp fast-action dried yeast
1 tsp salt
4 tsp caster sugar
1 large egg
zest of ½ orange

A couronne is a type of bread shaped into wreath or crown, and in this recipe the berries' tart sweetness is the perfect foil for the enriched dough. It is not difficult to make, and adds a bit of spectacle to your table. This version uses cranberry sauce – make it specially, or use leftovers from dinner.

METHOD

- **For the cranberry sauce**, put the cranberries in a small saucepan with the water and bring to a simmer. Cover, and simmer over a medium heat until the cranberries soften and burst. Remove from the heat and drain off the liquid. Push the berries through a sieve into a bowl; discard what is left in the sieve. Stir in the sugar until dissolved and leave to cool.
- **For the bread**, melt the butter into the milk in a saucepan over a low heat. Sift the flour into a large mixing bowl and add the yeast, salt and 1 tsp of the sugar (putting the yeast and salt on opposite sides of the bowl). Break in the egg, then pour in the milk/butter mixture. Combine the ingredients thoroughly, then knead until the dough is soft and silky (do all this by hand or using a stand mixer and dough hook – mix for 10 minutes). Cover and leave in a warm place for an hour, until the dough has doubled in size. Mix 4 tbsp of the cranberry sauce with the remaining sugar and orange zest and set aside. Flour a large surface and roll out the dough to a rectangle about 30 × 45cm/12 × 18in. Spread

the sauce mixture over the dough, leaving a 2cm/¾in border along one long edge. Roll up the dough as tightly as possible, starting from the long edge without the border, into a long sausage. Cut it in half along its length and lay side by side on the baking sheet with the cut sides uppermost. Weave the two halves over each other along their length, then shape into a wreath/circle. Tuck the loose ends under each other and press them together to form a complete circle. Cover and leave for a further hour in a warm place; meanwhile preheat the oven to 180°C/350°F/gas mark 4. Bake for 30 minutes, until the bread sounds hollow when tapped on the base. Remove from the oven and leave on a wire rack to cool. While the bread is still warm, brush it with the remaining cranberry sauce to glaze.

TO SERVE

Serve warm or cold, for breakfast.

GROW
Cranberries
(see page 80)

PUMPKINS & WINTER SQUASHES

These are both hard-skinned squashes harvested in autumn and have similar growing methods. They are interchangeable in recipes, so grow whichever you prefer to eat.

BEST VARIETIES

The winter squashes generally have a better flavour than true pumpkins: 'Crown Prince' is easily one of the best while others good for baking include 'Bonbon' and the more compact 'Honey Bear' and 'Uchiki Kuri'. Good pumpkin varieties are 'Tonda Padana' and 'Munchkin'.

PLANTING

Sow seeds under cover in spring, in modules or small pots. Harden off before planting out into a sunny spot in late spring/early summer once there is little risk of frost. The plants will produce long trailing vines, so make sure they have plenty of room to scramble about – allow 1.5m/5ft between plants and between rows. Pumpkins and winter squashes can be used as ground cover under tall, thin crops (such as climbing beans) that will not cast too much shade. They can also be grown in large pots; plant one per pot. To save space, the vines can be tied to a wigwam of canes, but the fruit will need supporting in little hammocks – old pairs of tights are good for this.

MAINTENANCE

Keep well-watered, and once the fruits start to ripen in late summer make sure they are not too shaded by leaves. Fruits can be raised off the soil on bricks or stones, to prevent them rotting if the weather is wet.

HARVEST

Cut fruits from the plant once they are coloured all over and sound hollow when tapped. Store in a dry, sunny spot (inside or out) to allow the skins to harden.

RIGHT Pumpkins and winter squashes come in all shapes, colours and sizes.

BAKE
Chilli chocolate mudcake
(see page 144)
Pumpkin pie (see facing page)
Pumpkin soda bread
(see page 164)

PUMPKIN PIE

SERVES 10–12

YOU WILL NEED
1 × flan tin, 23–25cm/9–10in
diameter, greased
1 × baking sheet

INGREDIENTS

Glazed pecans:
50g/2oz caster sugar
24 (plus a few spares) pecan
halves, toasted and cooled

Pastry case:
230g/8oz plain flour
pinch of salt
80g/2½oz unsalted butter,
chilled
80g/2½oz caster sugar
2 eggs, beaten

Filling:
300g/10oz roasted pumpkin
flesh, puréed
200ml/7fl oz double cream
2 eggs, beaten
150g/5oz caster sugar
½ tsp salt
1 tsp ground cinnamon
1 tsp ground ginger
1 tsp ground mixed spice

An autumn classic, this pie could be made with pumpkin
or winter squash, and is enhanced with warming spices
and sugared pecans.

METHOD

- **For the glazed pecans**, put the sugar in a small saucepan on
a medium heat and stir until you have a caramel liquid. Turn
the heat to as low as possible and, while working quickly, put
a few pecans in at a time, stir to coat them in the sugar then
scoop them out with a fork. Lay out to cool on a piece of
baking paper, making sure the nuts do not touch each other.
- **For the pastry case**, line the greased tin with the pastry. Trim
off the excess around the edge, and place in the refrigerator.
Preheat the oven to 200°C/400°F/gas mark 6, and place a
baking sheet on the middle shelf.
- **For the filling**, mix the pumpkin purée with the rest of the
ingredients thoroughly. Pour the filling into the pastry case (if
you do this once the case is on the baking sheet in the oven,
it will minimize the risk of spillages). Bake for 10 minutes, then
turn the oven down to 170°C/325°F/gas mark 3 and bake for
a further 30–40 minutes, until the filling wobbles only very
slightly in the middle when shaken. Remove the pie from the
oven, but leave it in the tin for 10 minutes before placing the
glazed pecans around the edge.

TO SERVE

Serve warm or cold, perhaps with a spoonful of whipped cream.

GROW
Pumpkins &
winter squashes
(see facing page)

GINGER

BAKE
Ginger cake
(see facing page)

Ginger's exotic, architectural foliage makes it a great houseplant, but its foliage can reach 1m/3ft tall, so make sure you have a suitable position for this frost-tender plant. In hot summers the pot can be moved outside once there is little risk of frost.

BEST VARIETIES

Culinary ginger is *Zingiber officinale*.

PLANTING

In temperate climates, ginger is best grown in a large pot in a greenhouse or on a windowsill, in dappled shade. While it is possible to buy potted plants, you could grow your own from a shop-bought root. Choose your root carefully – it should not be too dry, mouldy (any cut surfaces should have healed over) and there must be at least one little bud on it.

Fill a pot to within 2cm/¾in of the rim with gritty multipurpose compost mixed in a ratio of 1:3 grit to potting compost. Water it well. Then place the ginger root on the compost surface, press down to bed it in and cover with more compost.

MAINTENANCE

Keep the compost moist and warm (some heat from the base will help) until roots grow into the compost and shoots appear. Feed every two weeks during summer, and cut down old stems in autumn. Replant into a large pot and keep repotting as necessary: tall, deep pots are better than shallow, wide ones.

HARVEST

If you planted a ginger root in spring, you should be able to harvest in autumn, but the longer you grow the plant the more roots you will get. Unpot or dig up the plant and cut off the roots (remembering to save a piece to replant). The roots have the strongest flavour while the swollen ball at the base of the stem is the stem ginger – the part of the plant that is sold boiled in syrup.

LEFT A small pot is fine to start off a ginger plant, but move it to a bigger one as it grows.

GINGER CAKE

MAKES A SINGLE-LAYER CAKE

YOU WILL NEED

1 × deep, round cake tin, 20cm/8in diameter, greased and base-lined

INGREDIENTS

40g/1½oz peeled, finely grated
    and chopped fresh ginger root
150g/5oz finely grated potatoes
150g/5oz unsalted butter
150g/5oz dark brown muscovado sugar
100ml/3½fl oz black treacle
2 eggs
250g/8oz plain flour
1½ tsp ground ginger
1 tsp ground cinnamon
2 tsp baking powder

METHOD

- Preheat the oven to 160°C/325°F/gas mark 3. Combine the ginger root and potatoes and set aside.
- Beat the butter and sugar together until light and fluffy, then stir in the treacle. Add the eggs one at a time, beating well after each one. Stir in the ginger and potato mix.
- Combine the flour, spices and baking powder and sift into the mix. Fold in until everything is thoroughly incorporated.
- Bake for 50–55 minutes, until a skewer comes out clean. Remove from the oven and leave in the tin for 10 minutes, then turn out on to a wire rack to cool completely.

TO SERVE

Whenever your morning snack needs to be a serious pick-me-up.

If you are ambivalent about ginger as a flavour, this dark, gingery, treacly cake is probably not for you. Grate and chop the ginger root finely to ensure the fibres are not too long, as they will persist in the baked cake.

GROW

Ginger (see facing page)
Potatoes (see page 162)

RIGHT Ginger has attractive foliage and flowers as well as delicious roots.

GROW
Raspberries
(see page 64)

RASPBERRY & WHITE CHOCOLATE ROLL

SERVES 6–8

YOU WILL NEED

1 × Swiss roll tin, 20 × 30cm/
8 × 12in, greased, base-lined,
base and sides dusted with flour

INGREDIENTS

Sponge:
80g/2½oz plain flour
pinch of salt
3 eggs
80g/2½oz caster sugar
½ tsp vanilla extract
1 tbsp warm water
35–40 raspberries,
   defrosted if frozen
caster sugar, for sprinkling

Ganache:
65ml/2fl oz double cream
150g/5oz white chocolate

Filling and decoration:
150g/5oz raspberry jam
Icing sugar, to dust

This Swiss roll is studded with raspberries, giving it a polka-dot pattern. By using preserved raspberries – frozen or in jam form – it is possible to have a taste of summer even in the depths of winter. Usually a Swiss roll is turned out of the tin and then rolled, meaning the top of the sponge in the tin becomes the outside of the roll. Here the polka-dot pattern is usually better on the bottom of the sponge, so it needs flipping over once it is turned out, but omit this stage if the top of the sponge looks good.

METHOD

- **For the sponge**, preheat the oven to 170°C/325°F/gas mark 3. Mix the flour and salt together and set aside. Whisk the eggs and sugar together until they hold their shape and are very light and fluffy (they will approximately quadruple in volume). Add the vanilla extract and water, then sift in the flour and salt mixture. Using a large metal spoon, fold into a smooth batter, maintaining as much air in the mix as possible. Pour the batter into the tin. Stud raspberries into the mix (pointy end downwards), setting them in lines angled at about 30° to one of the long sides. Bake for 12–15 minutes until the sponge is firm to the touch and lightly browned. While it is baking, liberally sprinkle a large piece of baking paper with caster sugar. Remove the sponge from the oven and turn it out on to the sugared paper, and very carefully peel off the base liner by tearing a strip off at a time. If you want the underside as the roll's outside, sprinkle the exposed sponge with more caster sugar and immediately cover with another piece of baking paper. Holding the two sheets together tightly, flip the sponge over. Score a line through the sponge along one of the shorter sides, about 1cm/½in from the edge, then starting from this end roll up the sponge as tightly as possible. Leave to cool, rolled and wrapped in the paper, on a wire rack.
- **For the ganache**, bring the cream to just under the boil in a small saucepan over a medium heat, then pour it over the chocolate. Stir until melted and smooth, then set aside to cool to a spreading, but not runny, consistency.

TO ASSEMBLE

Unroll the cooled sponge, spread with the jam, then ganache, and reroll. Dust very lightly with icing sugar – do not obscure the spots! – and serve.

SWEET POTATOES

BAKE

Sweet potato &
marshmallow cake
(see facing page).

Although the sweet potatoes are the main crop at the end of the season, the plants also produce an extra harvest through the summer of edible leaves (like spinach) from their attractive climbing vines.

BEST VARIETIES

New varieties are being bred that will do better in a cool-temperate climate: try for example 'Georgia Jet' or 'T65'. 'O'Henry' is good for container growing. The sweetest variety is purple 'Okinawa'. If you find a variety in the shops that you like, buy another from which to grow your own plants (see below).

PLANTING

Like potatoes, sweet potatoes are grown using the previous year's tubers, but the shoots off the tuber (called slips) are planted rather than the tuber itself. These can be bought as unrooted slips or as plug plants from garden centres and online suppliers: if you get them sent through the post they will need rehydrating in a glass of water overnight.

Make your own slips, in spring, by inserting a whole sweet potato, upright with about half submerged, into a glass of water and putting it in a warm, sunny place. It will grow roots and then shoots. Once the shoots are about 20cm/8in long, snip them off. Plant your slips into tall, deep pots, submerging about half the stem in the compost. Place them in a warm, sunny spot and keep the compost moist while you wait for them to sprout roots.

Sweet potatoes will benefit from a long, warm summer. Ideally plant out your rooted slips/plug plants in a greenhouse or polytunnel, although a really sunny, warm and sheltered spot outside should also encourage a good harvest. Leave 30cm/12in between plants and 70cm/28in between rows.

These plants will do just as well in a large pot as in the ground, although they prefer free-draining soil, so mix in some sand or grit to the potting compost when cultivating them in pots.

MAINTENANCE

The top growth can be tied to canes or be left to scramble over the ground – it will make no difference to the size of the harvest. Keep plants well-watered and feed pot-grown plants.

HARVEST

Dig up the tubers in autumn after the first frost. They need to be cured before they can be used, so arrange them in a crate in a single layer, not touching. Cover the crate with a damp cloth (rewet it regularly). Place in a warm (21–25°C/70–77°F) room. After 2–4 weeks any scratches on their skins should have healed over, and they are ready to cook.

ABOVE Grow your own sweet potato slips by putting a shop-bought potato into a vase of water.

SWEET POTATO & MARSHMALLOW CAKE

MAKES A TWO-LAYER CAKE

YOU WILL NEED

2 × deep, round cake tins,
20cm/8in diameter, greased and
base-lined

INGREDIENTS

Mashed sweet potatoes:
800–900g/1lb 12oz–2lb
   sweet potatoes

Cake:
400g/14oz plain flour
1½ tbsp baking powder
¾ tsp salt
¼ tsp black pepper
½ nutmeg, finely grated,
   or ½ tsp ground nutmeg
165g/5½oz unsalted butter
250g/8oz light muscovado sugar
4 eggs
450g/1lb mashed
   sweet potatoes
90g/3oz mini-marshmallows

Ganache:
45ml/1½fl oz double cream
100g/3oz white chocolate

Decoration:
½ jar of marshmallow fluff
   (about 100g/3½oz)
100g/3½oz marshmallows

If sweet potato & marshmallow casserole, the traditional Thanksgiving dish, is too sweet for your turkey dinner, use this great pairing in cake form instead. It is perfect after a long winter's walk.

METHOD

- **For the mashed sweet potatoes**, preheat the oven to 180°C/350°F/gas mark 4. Roast the sweet potatoes for around 45 minutes until they are soft. Remove from the oven and leave to cool completely, then pop them out of their skins. Mash well (use a potato ricer if you have one).
- **For the cake**, preheat the oven to 170°C/325°F/gas mark 3. Combine the flour, baking powder, salt, pepper and nutmeg in a bowl and mix well; leave to one side. Beat the butter and sugar together until light and fluffy. Add the eggs, one at a time, beating well to incorporate after each egg. Mix in the mashed sweet potato, then the flour and spice mix. Quickly stir in the mini-marshmallows and divide the cake mixture between the two tins. Make sure that all the marshmallows on the surface are coated with mixture to prevent them burning. Bake for 50–60 minutes. To check if it is ready insert a skewer into the cake; if it comes out clean the cake is cooked. Remove from the oven and leave for 10 minutes in the tins, then turn out on to a wire rack to cool completely.
- **For the ganache**, heat the cream in a small saucepan over a medium heat until just under boiling point. Pour over the chocolate and stir until it has melted and is smooth. Leave to cool until the mixture is thick enough to spread without running.

TO ASSEMBLE

Sandwich the two cake layers together with the ganache, spread marshmallow fluff on the top and sprinkle with whole marshmallows.

GROW
Sweet potatoes
(see facing page)

GROW

Apples (see page 136)
Berries (see pages 64 and 106)
Currants (see pages 122 and 130)
Plums (see page 140)
Rhubarb (see page 54)
Sweet potatoes (see page 90)

A MUFFIN FOR ALL SEASONS

MAKES 12 MUFFINS

YOU WILL NEED

1 × 12-hole muffin or cupcake tin, lined with paper cases or greased

INGREDIENTS

Basic muffin batter:
- 350g/12oz plain flour
- 150g/5oz light brown muscovado sugar
- 2 tsp baking powder
- ½ tsp salt
- 100g/3½oz unsalted butter, melted and cooled
- 1 egg
- 300ml/½ pint milk
- 2 tbsp demerara sugar

SEASONAL FRUIT/VEG VERSIONS:

Rhubarb and ginger:
- 1 tsp ground ginger
- 100g/3½oz finely diced rhubarb

Summer berries:
- ½ tsp vanilla extract
- 250g/8oz soft fruit (blueberries, raspberries or currants)

Plum:
- ½ tsp vanilla extract
- 2 large plums, pitted and cut into 6 slices each

Apple and sweet potato:
- 1 tsp ground cinnamon
- 100g/3½oz grated sweet potato
- 100g/3½oz grated dessert apple

Add this basic batter mix to whatever fruit and vegetables are in season but be careful not to over-mix the muffins, or they will be chewy and dense rather than light and fluffy. Aim to combine everything with 10–20 stirring strokes.

METHOD

- **For the basic batter**, preheat the oven to 190°C/375°F/gas mark 5. Mix together the flour, sugar, baking powder and salt in one bowl, and the melted butter, egg and milk in another. Pour the wet mix into the dry ingredients and, using a whisk, stir briefly to combine everything, adding any fruit/veg along the way. Spoon into the prepared cases/tin and add any further fruit. Sprinkle the tops with a pinch of demerara sugar, if liked, and bake for 25 minutes until well-risen and springy to the touch. Remove from the oven and leave on a wire rack to cool.
- **For the rhubarb and ginger version**, add the ground ginger to the dry ingredients before mixing, and stir in the rhubarb halfway through combining the wet and dry ingredients.
- **For the summer berries version**, add the vanilla extract to the wet ingredients. Stir in two-thirds of the berries halfway through combining the wet and dry ingredients, and stud the remaining berries into the top of the batter once it is in the cases/tin holes.
- **For the plum version**, add the vanilla extract to the wet ingredients, and set 2 plum pieces into the top of each muffin once the batter is in the cases/tin holes.
- **For the apple and sweet potato version**, add the ground cinnamon to the dry ingredients. Stir in the sweet potato and apple halfway through combining the wet and dry ingredients.

TO ASSEMBLE

Serve for breakfast, if you are in a rush and/or feeling decadent, or for elevenses.

PARSNIPS

These vegetables get a bad press – in some countries they are grown only as animal feed – but they really do not deserve it. It is true they take up space in the veg patch for a while before they can be harvested, but the sweet roots are worth the wait, and make a great addition to the seasonal ingredients list.

BEST VARIETIES

'Tender and True' and 'Gladiator' are classics, and reliable. Baby parsnips such as 'Arrow' can be harvested early, in summer and early autumn.

PLANTING

As with all root crops, you will get the best roots in soils that are not too heavy or stony; parsnips also like an open, sunny position. Sow in spring, spacing rows 30cm/12in apart. Parsnips can also be grown in tall, deep pots. It is not necessary to make successional sowings if you do not have the space, because parsnips keep well in the ground until you want to harvest them. Germination will take quite a few weeks; by mixing fast-germinating radish seed with the parsnip seed, the radishes will show you where the row is (and give you a harvest of radishes meanwhile) before the parsnip seedlings get going. Thin to 15cm/6in between plants. (Use the thinnings in Root veg tarte Tatin, see page 169.)

MAINTENANCE

Keep weed-free and watered in dry spells.

HARVEST

Parsnips will be sweeter if they are harvested after the first frosts. Use a fork to lever the roots out of the ground as you need them, though they will store for a week or more in the refrigerator if you know the ground is going to be frozen solid at harvest time.

BAKE
Parsnip winter cake
(see facing page)
Root veg tarte Tatin
(see page 169)

RIGHT Parsnip seedlings will emerge just as the radishes marking the row are ready to harvest.

PARSNIP WINTER CAKE

Parsnips and honey pair together wonderfully in this lighter version of a fruit cake. It is worth getting the best honey you can afford – preferably local, produced by an artisan supplier – as it will impart real flavour as well as sweetness.

MAKES A SINGLE-LAYER CAKE

YOU WILL NEED
1 × deep, round cake tin, 20cm/8in diameter, greased and base-lined

INGREDIENTS
150g/5oz unsalted butter
150g/5oz light muscovado sugar
4 eggs
250g/8oz peeled parsnips, coarsely grated
100g/3½oz sultanas
50g/2oz chopped candied peel
200g/7oz plain flour
90g/3oz ground almonds
1 tsp ground ginger
½ tbsp baking powder
2 tbsp honey

METHOD
- Preheat the oven to 160°C/325°F/gas mark 3. Beat the butter and sugar together until light and fluffy, then beat in the eggs.
- Stir in the parsnips, sultanas and candied peel (by hand, or on a slow speed in a stand mixer).
- Sift in the flour, ground almonds, ground ginger and baking powder. Fold in by hand until everything is incorporated, then pour into the prepared tin and smooth level.
- Bake for around 1¼ hours, until a skewer inserted into the middle comes out clean. Remove from the oven and put the cake (still in the tin) on a cooling rack.
- Pierce about 12 holes in the cake, all the way to the base, with a skewer, and drizzle the honey over the top. Allow the cake to cool completely in the tin, before turning out.

TO SERVE
Serve with a hot cup of tea after a long walk on a cold day.

TOFFEE APPLE CUPCAKES

MAKES 12 CUPCAKES

YOU WILL NEED

1 × baking sheet, lined with baking paper
1 × 12-hole muffin or cupcake tin, lined with paper cases or greased

INGREDIENTS

Apple crisps:
100ml/3½fl oz water
2 tsp caster or granulated sugar
2 tsp lemon juice
1–2 dessert apples, thinly sliced from top to bottom

Cupcakes:
65g/2½oz unsalted butter
165g/5½oz (golden) caster sugar
150g/5oz peeled, cored and diced dessert apples
150g/5oz plain flour
4 tsp baking powder
pinch of salt
120ml/4fl oz milk
2 eggs
100g/3½oz coarsely grated dessert apple (no need to peel the apple)

Buttercream:
60g/2oz muscovado sugar
90ml/3fl oz double cream
115g/4oz unsalted butter
200g/7oz icing sugar

Make these for eating around a bonfire on a cold winter's night.

METHOD

- **For the apple crisps**, preheat the oven to 110°C/225°F/gas mark ¼. Bring the water, sugar and lemon juice to the boil in a saucepan, then take it off the heat. Add the apple slices a few at a time, making sure they are coated on both sides. Drain off the liquid and put the slices on to the baking sheet. Cook for 1–2 hours, checking regularly; remove from the oven when they are dry and crisp.
- **For the cupcakes**, melt 20g/¾oz of the butter with 2 tsp of the sugar in a frying pan over a medium heat, and add the diced apples. Cook for 5 or so minutes until caramelized, then leave to cool. Preheat the oven to 170°C/325°F/gas mark 3. Beat the remaining butter into all but 1 tbsp of the flour, baking powder and salt until it looks like sand. Stir in the remaining sugar, then add the milk and beat well. Add the eggs and beat well. Toss the caramelized diced apple in the reserved 1 tbsp of flour so that all the sides are coated. Stir in the grated apple by hand. Divide the mix between the 12 cases, sprinkle the tops with the caramelized diced apple and bake for 20–25 minutes. Remove from the oven and leave to cool in the tin for 5 minutes before taking out and leaving to cool completely on a wire rack.
- **For the buttercream**, put the muscovado sugar, cream and 15g/½oz of the butter in a saucepan over a low–medium heat, stirring to dissolve the sugar. Bring to the boil and then simmer for 4 minutes until slightly thickened, then leave the toffee sauce to cool. Beat the icing sugar and remaining butter together thoroughly, then pour in the toffee sauce and continue beating for 5–10 minutes until it is light and fluffy.

TO ASSEMBLE

Pipe the buttercream on top of the cupcakes and top each with an apple crisp.

GROW
Apples (see page 136)
Lemons (see page 119)

GROW
Apples (see page 136)
Pears (see page 146)
Plums (see page 140)

MINCE PIES

MAKES 48 MINCE PIES

YOU WILL NEED
1 × large baking dish
1 × 12-hole muffin or cupcake
    tin, greased
1 × cookie cutter, 11cm/4½in
    diameter
1 × cookie cutter, 10cm/4in
    diameter

INGREDIENTS

Mincemeat:
750g/1lb 10oz plums,
    halved and pitted
250g/8oz damsons,
    halved and pitted
zest and juice 2 large oranges
500g/1lb 2oz dessert apples,
    pears or a mix of these,
    peeled, cored and cut into
    1cm/½in cubes
600g/1lb 5oz sultanas
100g/3½oz marmalade
250g/8oz demerara sugar
½ tsp ground cloves
2 tsp ground ginger
½ nutmeg, finely grated
100g/3½oz almonds, chopped
50ml/1½fl oz amaretto
    liqueur

Pastry case:
350g/12oz plain flour
125g/4oz butter, chilled
125g/4oz caster sugar
2 eggs and an egg yolk

Decoration:
1 egg, beaten with a small
    pinch of salt
3–4 large pinches
    of demerara sugar

Everybody has their own holiday routines – those activities that signal the countdown can begin. Personally it is the spicy, fruity aroma of mincemeat that tells me (even though it is still autumn) that Christmas is not far away. This recipe uses fresh apples, plums and damsons, and owes its proportions to Pam Corbin's recipe in *River Cottage Handbook 2: Preserves*. Use the mincemeat to make Mince pies (see below), Mincemeat cookies (see page 118) or add a spoonful or two to an Apple pie (see page 138) or crumble, or to your morning porridge.

METHOD

- **For the mincemeat**, put the plums and damsons in a large saucepan with the orange juice. Cook gently until tender (15 minutes). Blend, or push through a sieve, to a purée. In a large baking dish mix 700ml/1¼ pints of the fruit purée with all the other ingredients except the amaretto; leave, covered, for 12 hours. Preheat the oven to 130°C/250°F/gas mark 1. Bake the mincemeat for 2½ hours. Mix in the amaretto, then spoon the mincemeat into warm, sterilized jars. It will keep for up to a year.
- **For the pastry case**, preheat the oven to 180°C/350°F/gas mark 4. Roll out the pastry as thinly as possible, and cut 12 discs using an 11cm/4½in cutter and 12 lids with a 10cm/4in cutter (you will need to reroll the trimmings to get enough). Transfer each disc to a hole in the prepared muffin tin, easing them in gently to fit the base and sides. Spoon the mincemeat (about 2 dessert spoonfuls per case) into the pastry cases, then lay a lid on each. Using a fork, press the edges of the base and lid together to seal.
- **For the decoration**, brush the top of each pastry case with the egg, then make two small cuts in the top of each to let the steam out. Sprinkle the tops with the demerara sugar, then bake for 20 minutes. Remove from the oven and ease the pies out of the tin, then leave them to cool on a wire rack.

AFTERNOON TEA

CHERRIES

The all-too-brief cherry season is something I look forward to every year, and I appreciate the fruit even more in the short time that it is available.

BAKE
Fresh fruit cake
(see page 66)
Black Forest bites
(see page 104)

BEST VARIETIES

Sweet cherries such as 'Stella' give a better range of possibilities than the sour (acid) varieties, but the sweet/sour cross 'May Duke' has an excellent flavour and is sweet enough to eat fresh too. Consider the practicalities as well – dwarf and trained fruit are easier to protect against the birds than large trees, so pick a suitable rootstock. If you have space for only one tree, make sure it is self-fertile ('Stella' is, and 'May Duke' is partially self-fertile); when planning to have more than one cherry tree, check that their pollination groups are compatible.

PLANTING

Cherry trees grow well in most soils providing there is good drainage. The site is important though: if the flowers get frosted in spring the crop will be lost for that year. A sheltered, south- or west-facing site is ideal, as is training against a wall. Plants can be bought potted or bare-root in the dormant season, and they can be grown as free-standing trees or as fans trained on a wall or fence. It is possible to buy trees that have been partially trained to start you off. For growing in pots, dwarf varieties are best.

MAINTENANCE

Stake free-standing cherry trees and those in pots. All trees benefit from being netted against birds once the fruit begins to ripen. Mulch annually, and water if it is dry when the tree is producing fruit – an irregular water supply can cause the fruit to split and be spoilt. Prune trees in summer (after harvesting), to avoid spreading a couple of cherry-specific diseases that are more easily transmitted in winter. Remove dead, diseased, damaged or duplicate wood, to maintain an open goblet framework in free-standing trees or to retain a good fan shape.

HARVEST

In summer, pick as the fruit reddens and ripens. You will need to go back to the tree at least twice, because cherries do not ripen evenly. To avoid pulling off the unripe fruit as well, you could cut the stalks with scissors.

LEFT Keep the stalk on each cherry as you pick it.
RIGHT Prune cherry trees in the summer, to avoid spreading diseases.

BLACK FOREST BITES

MAKES 12 BROWNIES

YOU WILL NEED

1 × mini-sponge tin, with holes of 4–5cm/1½–2in diameter, 12 holes minimum, greased, or 1 × 12-hole fairy cake tin lined with mini-fairy cake paper cases

INGREDIENTS

Brownies:
150g/5oz plain dark chocolate (70 per cent cocoa solids)
80g/2½oz unsalted butter, cubed
160g/5oz caster sugar
40g/1¼oz plain flour
2 eggs, beaten
12 cherries, pitted and stalks removed

Decoration:
40g/1½oz white chocolate, melted
12 cherries with stalks

There is a reason Black Forest gateau is enduringly popular: cherries and chocolate are made for each other. Inspired by that cake, these mini-brownies have a whole cherry baked within them, and another on top.

METHOD

- Preheat the oven to 170°C/325°F/gas mark 3. Melt the dark chocolate in a large bowl, then remove from the heat. Add the butter and stir until melted and the mixture is smooth. Add in the sugar, then the flour and egg until the mix is smooth.
- Put a teaspoonful of brownie mixture in the bottom of each hole in the tin. Set a cherry on top, then fill in with enough brownie mixture to bring it just below rim level.
- Bake for 15–20 minutes, until the tops are slightly domed and cracked. Remove from the oven and leave to cool completely in the tin, then pop out the brownies.

TO ASSEMBLE

Drizzle a little white chocolate over the brownies. Dip the base of a cherry into the remaining chocolate and place it carefully on the top of a brownie; repeat with the remaining cherries and brownies.

GROW

Cherries (see page 102)

STRAWBERRIES

There simply is no comparison between sun-warmed fruit picked and eaten straight away and the watery, flavourless offerings at the supermarket. Strawberries need so little to provide you with handfuls of gorgeous, red berries, and you will never have to buy another plant again.

BAKE

Fresh fruit cake (see page 66)
Fruity pizza (see page 142)
Strawberry & lemon sablés
(see page 120)
Shades of berry cake (see page 76)
Strawberry & basil cupcakes
(see facing page)
Strawberry tart
(see page 148)

BEST VARIETIES

For baking, it is best to choose the summer-fruiting varieties that bear all their fruit in one go, rather than the perpetual or 'everbear' types. It is still possible to get strawberry harvests throughout the summer by choosing early, mid- and late-season varieties such as 'Honeoye', 'Cambridge Favourite' and 'Symphony' respectively. Avoid the insipid 'Elsanta' at all costs.

PLANTING

Strawberries will grow in most soils but need a sunny position for the fruit to ripen well. Buy plants in pots and plant in autumn or early spring. When planting, ensure that the 'crown' – that part of the plant where all the stems and roots join – is at soil level. If it is buried the plant is likely to rot away, and if it is not deep enough it will probably dry out and die. Put no more than three plants in a 30cm/12in-diameter pot, otherwise they will become overcrowded.

MAINTENANCE

Make sure the soil or compost is consistently moist, especially as the fruit starts to develop, or the berries will be misshapen. Give potted plants a liquid feed every two weeks. Surround plants grown in beds and borders with straw as the fruit begins to ripen – this will keep the berries off the soil and they will be cleaner. It may be necessary to protect your strawberry plants with netting to prevent marauding birds, squirrels and/or mice. Pots are easier to move – my strawberries have to be out of reach of the dog, which is partial to the fruit.

Replace strawberry plants every 2–3 years. For free replacement plants, root the first little plantlet on a runner (long trailing stems produced as the plant finishes fruiting) into its own pot by pinning it down (half a paperclip works well) into moist compost. Cut off the rest of the runner beyond the plantlet but leave it attached to the mother plant until it has developed its own roots. Root only the first plantlet per runner, and no more than two per mother plant.

HARVEST

Pick the fruit as it ripens, leaving the strawberries until they are the deepest red for the best flavour. Remove as much of the stalk with each fruit as possible, as stubs left on the plant are liable to rot.

ABOVE Pin runners into separate pots, to create new plants for free.

STRAWBERRY & BASIL CUPCAKES

MAKES 12 CUPCAKES

YOU WILL NEED
1 × 12-hole muffin or cupcake tin, lined with paper cases or greased

INGREDIENTS

Cupcakes:
180g/6oz plain flour
2½ tsp baking powder
small pinch of salt
60g/2oz unsalted butter
160g/5½oz caster sugar
2 eggs
125ml/4fl oz milk
150g/5oz strawberries,
  cut into small dice

Frosting:
7 basil leaves
90g/3oz butter
2½ tbsp double cream
250g/8oz icing sugar
green food colouring (optional)

Decoration:
12 strawberries
12 sprigs/leaves of basil

Strawberries pair well with all sorts of unexpected flavours and are very good with a hint of basil, supplied here in the frosting.

METHOD

- **For the cupcakes**, preheat the oven to 170°C/325°F/gas mark 3. Set aside 1 tbsp of the flour. Sift the remaining flour, the baking powder and salt into a bowl and mix together. Add the butter and beat with a paddle attachment (or rub in by hand) until the mixture resembles breadcrumbs. Stir in the sugar. Whisk the eggs into the milk briefly, and beat into the dry mix until everything is combined, then beat on a medium-high setting for 2 minutes. Spoon into the paper cases or individual tin holes. Toss the strawberry pieces in the reserved flour and scatter over the tops of the cakes. Bake for 25 minutes. Remove from the oven and cool for 5 minutes in the tin before turning out on to a wire rack to cool completely.
- **For the frosting**, tear up the basil leaves then blend them with 25g of the butter and the cream. Sift the icing sugar into a bowl, add the remaining butter and the basil butter (and a few drops of green food colouring if liked). Beat until fluffy (for 5 minutes or more on a high setting).

TO ASSEMBLE
Pipe the frosting on to the cooled cupcakes and top with a strawberry and basil leaf. Serve straight away.

GROW
Basil (see page 109)
Strawberries
(see facing page)

RIGHT Strawberry flowers are also edible and can be used as decoration.

BEETROOT BROWNIES

MAKES 16–20 SMALL SQUARES

YOU WILL NEED

1 × brownie or shallow roasting tin, 20 × 25 × 3cm/8 ×10 × 1¼in, base- and side-lined

INGREDIENTS

200g/7oz plain dark chocolate (70 per cent cocoa solids), broken into small pieces
125g/4oz unsalted butter, cubed
200g/7oz caster sugar
300g/10oz cooked, peeled and finely grated beetroot
150g/5oz plain flour
3 tbsp cocoa powder
3 eggs
1 tsp vanilla extract
pinch of sea-salt flakes (optional)
icing sugar, to dust

METHOD

- Preheat the oven to 170°C/325°F/gas mark 3. Melt the chocolate in a large bowl. Then remove the bowl from the heat and stir in the butter until melted and the mixture is smooth. Stir in the sugar, then the beetroot, then sift in the flour and cocoa powder and stir again until incorporated.
- Beat the eggs with the vanilla extract then add to the mix, stirring until everything is fully incorporated and smooth.
- Pour into the prepared tin. If you like the combination of salt and chocolate (I am aware not everyone does), sprinkle a few flakes over the top.
- Bake for 30 minutes, when cracks will appear on the top. Remove from the oven and leave to cool completely in the tin.

TO SERVE

Cut into squares and dust with icing sugar.

Beetroot and chocolate are a classic combination. Here the beetroot makes the brownies even squidgier, and replaces some of the usual amount of butter so you can justify that second portion.

BELOW Harvest beetroot before it gets too large and woody.

GROW
Beetroot (see page 58)

HERBS

Herbs are invaluable for attracting pollinating insects to your other crops, and their scents can deter pests. Even if you do not actually bake with them, the fresh leaves and flowers make excellent cake decorations.

BASIL

BEST VARIETIES

The basils generally used in cooking are annual varieties such as sweet basil (*Ocimum basilicum* – try 'Sweet Genovese'), or Greek basil (*O. minimum*), which has a smaller habit and leaves. There are also a number of culinary basils with different scents, such as lemon, lime and cinnamon.

BAKE

Pesto potato scones
(see page 163)
Strawberry & basil
cupcakes (see page 107)

PLANTING

Basil prefers the sunniest spot available and well-drained soil, and also grows very happily in a pot. Sow seeds in spring, under cover, and plant out once there is little risk of frost. Alternatively buy young plants and plant out after the last frost. Supermarket pots of herbs are actually many individual plants in one pot. Given some care and attention they can make the transition to the herb bed outside for the summer, but divide the root ball into 2–4 sections to give the growing plants more space.

MAINTENANCE

Water as required and feed regularly. Keep pinching out the tips, even if you do not need them in the kitchen, to encourage bushy growth. Dispose of the plant once it has died off in autumn.

HARVEST

Gather the leaves from spring to autumn.

LEMON VERBENA

BEST VARIETIES

Aloysia citrodora has sweet but strong lemony leaves and tiny, pale purple flowers in summer.

PLANTING

Lemon verbena is not frost hardy, so can be best in a large pot that can be moved under cover in autumn and put back outdoors after the last frost in spring. Alternatively plant in the warmest, sunniest spot in the garden, ensuring the soil has good drainage. Buy lemon verbena in a pot and plant in spring. If it flourishes, it could reach up to 3m/10ft high and across.

MAINTENANCE

Cut back the stems to two buds above the old wood in spring, to keep its size in check. Give a good mulch in autumn. The branches may die back (cut them off in spring), but it should shoot again from the base (this may not be until early summer).

HARVEST

Pick the leaves from spring to autumn.

BAKE

Flower meringues
(see page 126)

MINT

BEST VARIETIES

There are many different scented mints. Spearmint (*Mentha spicata*) has fresh, bright green leaves good for decoration. However, the more pungent peppermint (*Mentha × piperita*) and chocolate mint (*M. × piperita* f. *citrata* 'Chocolate') are the best choices for baking with.

PLANTING

Mint plants will happily grow in a little shade. They tolerate most soils, but prefer moist soil to a free-draining one. Potted plants can be bought and planted year-round, but spring is the best time for doing this. Mint plants are rampant, and given the opportunity will spread through an entire bed, so growing the plants in large pots can be the best option. Alternatively plant 40cm/16in apart in the soil in a plunged pot, which will prevent the mint spreading. If the lip of the pot sits slightly above soil level, the roots (actually stolons) will be forced over it in their quest to find new soil. Snip them off around the pot's circumference on a regular basis to keep the plant contained.

MAINTENANCE

Mint flowers in midsummer if not regularly harvested, and the leaves then become straggly and dull. Cut all the growth back to ground level, and it will put on a second flush of fresh stems before dying back in autumn. Then remove the dead stems before new growth appears in spring.

HARVEST

Gather the leaves as needed through spring and summer, cutting the stem back to above a node each time.

BAKE

Chocolate herb tarts
(see page 112)
Mint choc-chip cupcakes
(see page 114)
Strawberry tart
(see page 148)

ROSEMARY

BEST VARIETIES

The main culinary form is *Rosmarinus officinalis*, but any rosemary can be used in the kitchen.

PLANTING

Rosemary needs well-drained soil – add grit to potting compost if you are growing it in a pot – and a position in full sun with 1.25m/4ft between plants. It is available as a potted plant, which can be bought and planted year-round, but ideally in spring.

MAINTENANCE

Water while the rosemary is establishing or if it is very dry (this especially applies to pot-grown plants), but overwatering and feeding will lead to lots of growth but weaker-flavoured leaves. Regular snipping of the shoots to use in the kitchen is all the pruning this shrub needs (cut stems evenly around the plant) and will also encourage bushy growth. However it will become woody and straggly over time, and is best replaced after 3–5 years.

HARVEST

Strip the leaves from the cut stems to use year-round. The tiny blue flowers appear in spring, and are delicately scented.

BAKE

Chocolate herb tarts
(see page 112)
Hazelnut & rosemary
pavlova (see page 153)

SCENTED PELARGONIUM

BEST VARIETIES

There are hundreds of varieties of geraniums (*Pelargonium*), in a wide range of different scents. By far the best are those with the citrus-perfumed leaves (lemon, orange, lime) and the rose-scented pelargoniums (e.g. *P.* 'Attar of Roses'), but there are also for example cinnamon and hazelnut fragrances.

PLANTING

Pelargoniums are frost tender, so in a cool-temperate climate they fare best in a pot that can be kept on a windowsill year-round or be moved outside for summer. They prefer to be in full sun and well-drained soil. Buy potted plants (source named varieties from specialist growers online or at plant fairs) and plant in spring.

MAINTENANCE

Make sure pelargoniums have enough water, but do not let them sit in soggy compost. Feed regularly from spring to late summer. Pull off old flower stems and yellowed leaves; these can be snapped cleanly from the main stem by hand, a therapeutic and satisfying task for a spare 5 minutes. Cut back all stems to a short, stubby framework in spring, to encourage fresh, new growth.

HARVEST

Pick leaves as required throughout the year.

BAKE
Flower meringues
(see page 126)

BAKE
Chocolate herb tarts
(see page 112)
Rose cake
(see page 73)

FAR LEFT Spearmint is good for decorating cakes.
LEFT Evergreen rosemary looks good all year round.
RIGHT Thyme flowers have a more delicate taste than the leaves.

THYME

BEST VARIETIES

Thymus vulgaris is the common thyme; use *T.* 'Culinary Lemon' for lemon thyme.

PLANTING

Thyme needs well-drained soil – add grit to potting compost if you are growing it in a pot – and a position in full sun, with 40cm/16in between plants. Potted plants can be bought and planted year-round, but spring is the best time for doing this.

MAINTENANCE

Maintain as for rosemary (see facing page).

HARVEST

Cut the shoots to use the leaves year-round, and the pink/purple flowers when they appear in early summer.

GROW

Mint (see page 110)
Rosemary (see page 110)
Thyme (see page 111)

CHOCOLATE HERB TARTS

MAKES 12 SMALL TARTLETS

YOU WILL NEED
1 × 12-hole fairy cake tin, greased;
1 × cookie cutter, 9cm/3½in
   diameter

INGREDIENTS

Pastry:
   120g/4½oz plain flour
   40g/1½oz unsalted butter,
      chilled
   40g/1½oz caster sugar
   1 egg

Ganache filling:
   200ml/7fl oz double cream
   80g/2½oz light brown
      muscovado sugar
   6–8 large sprigs rosemary or
      thyme or 4–6 large leaves
      mint (peppermint, chocolate
      mint, etc.)
   200g/7oz plain dark chocolate,
      broken into small pieces
      (70 per cent cocoa solids)

Decoration:
   cocoa powder (optional)
   herb sprigs (optional)

The herbs here enhance the chocolate beautifully in these little tarts of creamy ganache and crisp pastry.

METHOD
- **For the pastry**, make and blind bake 12 small tartlet cases. Leave to cool.
- **For the ganache**, put the cream and sugar in a small saucepan with the herbs and bring to the boil, stirring to dissolve the sugar. Simmer for 2 minutes, then remove from the heat and leave to cool. Bring the cream mix almost back to the boil and pour through a sieve over the chocolate. Stir well until all the chocolate has melted and the ganache is smooth and glossy. Spoon or pipe the ganache into the pastry cases and leave to cool.

TO SERVE
The tarts look attractive left as they are, but you could dust them with cocoa powder for an extra chocolate hit, or scatter a few leaves of the same herbs used in the ganache over the top.

MINT CHOC-CHIP CUPCAKES

MAKES 12 CUPCAKES

YOU WILL NEED

1 × 12-hole muffin or cupcake tin, lined with paper cases or greased

INGREDIENTS

Cupcakes:

4–5 large mint leaves
  (e.g. chocolate mint)
125ml/4fl oz semi-skimmed
  milk
180g/6oz plain flour
2½ tsp baking powder
small pinch of salt
60g/2oz unsalted butter
160g/5½oz caster sugar
2 eggs
100g/3½oz plain dark
  chocolate (70 per cent
  cocoa solids), finely chopped

Frosting:

16 large mint leaves
  (e.g. peppermint)
100g/3½oz caster sugar
100ml/3½fl oz water
225g/7½oz icing sugar
90g/3oz unsalted butter
green food colouring (optional)

Decoration:

plain dark chocolate shavings
12 sprigs/leaves of mint
  (e.g. peppermint or
  chocolate mint)

The advantage of growing your own mint is that you can choose which type to put into these cupcakes. I think they are best when chocolate mint infuses the sponge and peppermint the frosting, but try your own combinations.

METHOD

- **For the cupcakes,** put the mint leaves and milk into a saucepan and bring to the boil over a medium heat, then cover and set aside to cool. Preheat the oven to 170°C/325°F/ gas mark 3. Sift the flour, baking powder and salt into a bowl and mix together. Add the butter and beat with a paddle attachment on a stand mixer (or rub in by hand) until the mixture resembles breadcrumbs. Stir in the sugar. Remove the mint leaves from the milk and briefly whisk in the eggs. Beat into the dry mix until everything is combined, then mix on a medium–high setting for 2 minutes. Spoon into the cases or tin holes and scatter with the chopped chocolate. Bake for 25 minutes. Remove from the oven and leave for 5 minutes in the tin, then turn out on to a wire rack to cool completely.
- **For the frosting,** follow the flower syrup instructions in Flower meringues (see page 126) to make a mint syrup using the mint leaves, caster sugar and water. Set aside to cool, then remove the leaves. Sift the icing sugar into a bowl, add the butter and beat until combined. Still beating slowly, add the mint syrup in a slow drizzle, checking the intensity regularly and stopping when it is minty enough for you. Add a few drops of green food colouring if liked, and beat until fluffy (for 5 minutes or more on a high setting on a stand mixer).

TO ASSEMBLE

Pipe or spoon the frosting on to the cooled cupcakes and top with the chocolate shavings and a sprig of mint. Serve straight away.

GROW

Mint (see page 110)

TOMATOES

Using tomatoes to bake with is not that strange: a sun-warmed, ripe cherry tomato straight from the plant is sweetness itself.

BEST VARIETIES

Some of the sweetest varieties are cherry tomatoes such as yellowy orange 'Sungold' or red 'Gardener's Delight'. These are both cordon types, but cherry tomatoes can also be grown on a windowsill: 'Tumbling Tom' or 'Red Robin' are small bushy plants that nonetheless produce plenty of tomatoes in a single pot.

PLANTING

Sow seeds under cover in early spring, and plant out into the ground or a large pot in full sun (or in a greenhouse) in early summer after the last frost. Tomatoes will grow well in most soils. Alternatively buy young plants from a garden centre or local market, but the quality can be variable, and the choice of variety limited.

MAINTENANCE

Secure cordon tomato varieties to strong supports, at least 1.25m/4ft high, using figure-of-eight ties. Pinch out the side shoots as they appear and stop the growth by pinching out the tip of the plant once it reaches the top of the support. Bushy varieties do not need pinching out. Water to keep the soil evenly moist: irregular water supply can cause the fruit's skin to split. Using a proprietary tomato fertilizer or seaweed extract every two weeks once the first tiny fruits appear.

HARVEST

Gather the fruits as they ripen in summer. If outdoor plants still have fruit on them in late summer/early autumn and frost is forecast, cut off the whole truss and put in a warm place indoors to ripen (adding a ripe banana nearby will significantly help the ripening process). Avoid storing tomatoes in the refrigerator as this drastically reduces their flavour.

BAKE
Tomato cupcakes
(see facing page)

ABOVE On cordon tomatoes, pinch out the side shoots, which grow in the join between the leaves and main stem.

TOMATO CUPCAKES

MAKES 12 CUPCAKES

YOU WILL NEED

1 × 12-hole muffin or cupcake tin, lined with paper cases or greased

INGREDIENTS

Cupcakes:
2 eggs
150g/5oz light brown muscovado sugar
100ml/3½oz sunflower oil
200g/7oz plain flour
2 tsp baking powder
1 tsp ground cinnamon
¼ tsp freshly grated nutmeg
½ tsp salt
200g/7oz ripe, puréed tomatoes (preferably cherry tomatoes)

Frosting:
350g/12oz icing sugar
25g/1oz unsalted butter
150g/5oz cream cheese
1 tsp vanilla extract

Decoration:
ground cinnamon, to dust

These cupcakes bring back a spot of warmth to those rainy summer days, as the leaves start to signal that autumn is on its way.

METHOD

- **For the cupcakes**, preheat the oven to 170°C/325°F/gas mark 3. Whisk the eggs and sugar together until they are light and airy, then whisk in the oil for another two minutes. Mix together the flour, baking powder, spices and salt, then sift into the egg/sugar batter. Fold in until the dry ingredients are half-incorporated, then add the tomatoes and continue folding until the batter is smooth. Spoon into the cases or tin holes and bake for 20–25 minutes until a skewer comes out clean. Remove from the oven and leave in the tin for 5 minutes, then transfer to a wire rack and cool completely.
- **For the frosting**, sift the icing sugar, then add the butter, cream cheese and vanilla extract and beat for 5–7 minutes until smooth and creamy.

TO SERVE

The cupcakes look good with just a spoonful of frosting on top and some of the cake still showing. If you want to pipe the frosting, it can help to chill it in the refrigerator. Serve the frosted cupcakes with a dusting of ground cinnamon.

GROW
Tomatoes
(see facing page)

RIGHT Pick tomatoes on the vine where possible as they will keep for longer.

CARROT COOKIES

MAKES ABOUT 40 COOKIES

YOU WILL NEED

2 × baking sheets, lined with baking paper

INGREDIENTS

Cookie dough:
250g/8oz unsalted butter
125g/4oz caster sugar
1 egg yolk
250g/8oz plain flour
50g/1½oz porridge oats

COOKIE FILLING SUGGESTIONS:

Carrot and ginger filling:
200g/7oz peeled and
    finely grated carrots
½ tsp ground cinnamon
½ tsp ground ginger

Mincemeat filling:
200g/7oz mincemeat

Fresh berries filling:
40 fresh berries (e.g.
    raspberries, blueberries)

Icing:
150g/5oz icing sugar
juice from a handful of finely
    grated carrot (squeeze out
    by hand) or juice of a lemon

GROW

Blueberries (see page 74)
Carrots (see page 50)
Lemons (see facing page)
Raspberries
(see page 64)

These moreish, little cookies are a bit like the biscuit equivalent of carrot cake, and are the perfect accompaniment to a cup of tea. The dough can also be adapted to make mincemeat cookies (see Mince pies, page 98, for the mincemeat recipe), or it can even be shaped into little balls into which a fresh berry can be pressed before baking.

METHOD

- **For the cookie dough**, cream together the butter and sugar until light and fluffy. Add the egg yolk and beat again, then the flour and oats and mix until everything is incorporated.
- **For the carrot and ginger or mincemeat biscuit filling**, toss the carrots in the spices. Roughly fold the carrot mix or mincemeat into the biscuit dough, then turn it out on to a clean, floured surface and knead thoroughly (it will be quite sticky). Divide into two, roll each piece into a sausage shape, about 30cm/12in long, and wrap in clingfilm. For figuratively triangular-shaped carrot cookies, mould the sausage into a triangular prism. Chill the dough in the refrigerator for at least an hour, or overnight. Preheat the oven to 160°C/325°F/gas mark 3. Slice the dough into cookies, 1cm/½in thick, and set on to the baking sheet (they will not spread much). Bake for 18–20 minutes until light golden brown. Remove from the oven and leave on the tray for 5 minutes, then transfer to a wire rack to cool completely.
- **For the fresh berries biscuit filling**, turn the biscuit dough out on to a clean, floured surface and knead thoroughly. Divide into two, roll each piece into a sausage shape about 30cm/12in long and wrap in clingfilm. Chill the dough in the refrigerator for at least an hour, or overnight. Preheat the oven to 160°C/325°F/gas mark 3. Slice the dough into discs, 1cm/½in thick, then roll each disc into a ball. Put them on the baking sheet. Then make a dip in the top of each ball, with your thumb, and place a berry in it. Bake for 18–20 minutes until light golden brown. Remove from the oven and leave on the tray for 5 minutes, then transfer to a wire rack to cool completely.
- **For the icing**, sift the icing sugar into a bowl and add the carrot or lemon juice a few drops at a time until the icing comes together to an opaque but runny consistency.

TO SERVE

Drizzle the icing over the cookies.

LEMONS

To my mind, lemon trees are worth growing for the fragrance of their flowers alone. The fruit is a delicious bonus and worth treasuring in a recipe that allows it to shine, such as the Strawberry & lemon sablés (see page 120).

BEST VARIETIES

Lemon trees are *Citrus* × *limon*. The variety 'Meyer' is a compact tree.

PLANTING

Buy these frost-tender trees at any time of year, and plant into large pots; grow outside in the ground only if the temperatures never drop below 5°C/41°F. Give lemon trees the sunniest spot outside during summer once the night-time temperatures are warm enough. As the temperatures drop again, cover the plants with horticultural fleece at night until they need to be brought back under cover in autumn. Under cover, position in a frost-free but light area such as a greenhouse or conservatory. Centrally heated rooms are not ideal, as the air tends to be too dry – mist the foliage regularly if this is your only option.

MAINTENANCE

Water regularly during spring and summer, but restrict watering through the winter to only when the compost feels dry a few centimetres from the surface and feed through the growing season. Mist to help flowering plants set fruit. Repot in spring, replacing as much compost as possible, even if the plant goes back into the same pot. Lemons do not really need pruning, but pinching out the very tip of the branches in spring will encourage bushy growth.

HARVEST

Plants can flower and fruit at the same time, and year-round, so pick the lemons as they ripen.

BAKE

Apple pie (see page 138)
Carrot cake (see page 52)
Carrot cookies (see facing page)
Courgette cake (see page 62)
Pea cheesecake (see page 160)
Strawberry & lemon sablés
(see page 120)

ABOVE Horticultural fleece will protect lemons from a light frost.

GROW
Lemons (see page 119)
Strawberries
(see page 106)

STRAWBERRY & LEMON SABLÉS

MAKES 20–24 SABLÉS

YOU WILL NEED

2 × baking sheets, lined with baking paper
1 × heart-shaped or round cookie cutter, 3–4cm/1¼–1½in diameter

INGREDIENTS

Biscuits:
200g/7oz unsalted butter
100g/3½oz icing sugar
1 tsp vanilla extract
300g/10½oz plain flour
15g/½oz caster sugar
pinch of salt
icing sugar, for dusting

Lemon curd:
1 lemon, zest and juice
25g/1oz butter, diced
50g/2oz caster sugar
1 egg, beaten

Filling and topping:
1 tsp freeze-dried strawberries
½ tsp icing sugar
20–24 fresh strawberries

These cute little stacks of biscuits, fresh strawberries and zingy lemon curd are just the thing for afternoon tea. The butter biscuit (sablé) recipe comes from my husband's Swiss grandmother, while the inspiration for the strawberry sugar topping is from Heston Blumenthal.

METHOD

- **For the biscuits**, beat the butter and icing sugar together until light and fluffy. Add the vanilla extract and sift in the remaining ingredients and beat again until the mix comes together as a dough. Shape into a ball, flatten to a disc, wrap in clingfilm and put in the refrigerator for 1½ hours (or overnight). Preheat the oven to 160°C/325°F/gas mark 3. Dust a clean surface with icing sugar, and roll out the dough to 0.5cm/¼in thick. Cut out at least 60–72 biscuits and place on the baking sheets (you may need to bake them in a couple of batches). Bake for 10–15 minutes until they are lightly golden. Then remove from the oven and transfer to a wire rack to cool.
- **For the lemon curd**, put all of the ingredients in a bowl set over a pan of simmering water. Stir continuously for about 15 minutes, until the mixture is smooth and thick. It should leave an opaque coating on the back of a spoon – running a finger through it will leave a track. Remove from the heat and leave to cool. To store it for a week or two, pour into a warm, sterilized jar and keep in the refrigerator.
- **For the filling and topping**, crush the freeze-dried strawberries with the icing sugar (in a pestle and mortar or similar) and set this strawberry sugar aside. Slice the tops off the fresh strawberries, then cut into two thick, flat slices lengthways, discarding (eating!) the ends.

TO ASSEMBLE

Assemble into stacks of biscuit, lemon curd, strawberry slice, biscuit, lemon curd, strawberry slice, biscuit. Dust the tops with the strawberry sugar. Serve immediately.

REDCURRANTS

BAKE
Currant friands
(see facing page)
Fresh fruit cake (see page 66)
Fruity pizza
(see page 142)

Soft fruit bushes are a great investment. Within a couple of years you will have plenty of currants for making cakes, desserts and jam every summer, for the price of a couple of tiny punnets of fruit. Like gooseberries, fresh redcurrants are less widely available to buy. White- and pinkcurrants are grown in exactly the same way, and are even harder to find fresh in the shops.

BEST VARIETIES

'Jonkheer van Tets' and 'Stanza' are easily the best redcurrants – the former flowering and fruiting early in the season, and the latter in mid- to late summer. Of the whitecurrants try 'Versailles Blanche', and for pinkcurrants 'Gloire de Sablons' or 'Pink Champagne'.

PLANTING

Redcurrants crop well in partial shade, and they grow in any soil. Plant pot-grown bushes in autumn or spring, and bare-root plants in late autumn to early spring. Space 1.25m/4ft apart to grow as a bush. Alternatively train them as cordons 45cm/18in apart, against a wall or fence, or as fans 1.5m/5ft apart. Although it is possible to grow redcurrants in a large pot, when doing this it would be best to train them as a cordon against a stake.

MAINTENANCE

Mulch redcurrant bushes in spring. Prune bush plants to maintain a goblet shape of 8–10 branches by removing older, dead or diseased branches back to the main stem in early spring and by shortening new growth by one-half in midsummer. Cordons should have all new growth shortened to 5 buds in summer, then reduced back to 1 bud in winter. To prune a fan, treat each branch as if it were a cordon.

HARVEST

In summer, once the strings of currants shine red like little jewels among the foliage. Leave them for a couple of days after they turn red to ripen fully – you may want to net the plants to avoid having your harvest stolen by birds. It is easier to pick the entire string off the plant, then separate the currants from the stalk by running it through a fork.

CURRANT FRIANDS

Friands, little almond cakes, work well with most soft fruit: a single raspberry or gooseberry; a slice of plum or fig; or a scattering of black- or redcurrants, as here. The batter can be prepared quickly and easily (you will not need a stand mixer), and the friands do not take long to bake, so they are ideal when you fancy a little afternoon treat.

MAKES 12 FRIANDS

YOU WILL NEED

1 × 12-hole muffin or cupcake tin, greased

INGREDIENTS

100g/3½oz plain flour
200g/7oz icing sugar
150g/5¼oz ground almonds
6 egg whites
180g/6oz unsalted butter, melted
25g/1oz redcurrants

METHOD

- Preheat the oven to 180°C/350°F/gas mark 4. Sift the flour, sugar and ground almonds together into a large bowl, then make a well in the centre. Whisk the egg whites (by hand) until frothy, then pour into the well, followed by the butter. Fold everything together lightly.
- Spoon the batter into the tin holes, and very lightly stud the top of each friand with redcurrants.
- Bake for 20 minutes until the tops are pale golden and springy. Remove from the oven and leave in the tin for 5 minutes, then turn out on to a wire rack.

TO SERVE

Serve warm from the oven. Friands will keep for only 24 hours.

GROW
Redcurrants
(see facing page)

EDIBLE FLOWERS

Using flowers in the kitchen is something akin to alchemy for me: I love being able to bottle a syrup that tastes just like the fragrance in a rose garden, or savour the scent of lavender in a biscuit. There are many more flowers that are beautiful additions to the decoration of a cake, and these are listed below too.

LAVENDER

BAKE
Flower meringues
(see page 126)
Lavender shortbread
(see page 128)

BEST VARIETIES

When cooking use only the flowers of lavender (*Lavandula angustifolia*) or lavandin (*L. × intermedia*), or a variety thereof, such as the compact *L. angustifolia* 'Hidcote' or deep purple *L.a.* 'Imperial Gem'. **The flowers of *L. stoechas* (French lavender) are poisonous.**

PLANTING

Lavender prefers well-drained soil in full sun. Buy potted plants at any time of year, but the best time to plant is spring. Space 50cm/20in apart – closer if planting as a low hedge. This herb can also be grown successfully in pots.

MAINTENANCE

Hard pruning every summer is essential to preventing straggly, woody, unattractive growth. When the plants have finished flowering, find the point on each stem where it turns from green to brown, and cut back to there, just above a node.

HARVEST

Cut and use the flowers fresh while still in bud, or else dry them before they open by tying the stems in small bunches and hanging them upside-down in a warm, dry place. When completely dry, rub off the flower buds, spread them out on a piece of newspaper and leave for another couple of days before sealing the flowers in an airtight container to keep for up to a year.

LEFT Prune lavender where the stem turns from green to brown.

LEFT When harvesting roses, cut the stem just above a leaf, to encourage new shoots.

ROSES

BEST VARIETIES

While it is possible to use any rose flower in the kitchen, the best by far for flavour are pink apothecary's rose (*Rosa gallica* var. *officinalis*), prickly hedgehog rose (*Rosa rugosa*), which has deep pink flowers, or white-flowered *Rosa rugosa* 'Alba'.

BAKE
Flower meringues
(see page 126)
Rose cake
(see page 72)

PLANTING

Give roses a sunny spot and ensure their soil has had plenty of organic matter incorporated. Plant potted shrubs in spring, or bare-root ones in autumn to early spring. Allow 1m/3ft between plants of apothecary's rose, and 2–2.5m/7–8ft between hedgehog roses. Roses can be grown in large pots – apothecary's rose, being smaller, would be a good choice.

MAINTENANCE

Prune in early spring, as the buds just start to break, to remove dead, diseased or damaged wood, or weak growth, leaving a framework of healthy branches. Mulch after pruning and water in very dry spells.

HARVEST

Cut the flowers as needed during summer – regular picking and deadheading of unused flowers will promote more flowering. When harvesting rose flowers, cut back the stem to a strong, outward-facing bud rather than leaving an ugly little stub. This will encourage more branching and flowering.

ELDERFLOWERS

I am not detailing the cultivation of common elder (*Sambucus nigra*) here because it is so ubiquitous in hedgerows, both rural and urban, and fun to forage for. Pick the large, white, umbel flowers in late spring and early summer, avoiding trees in dusty areas such as roadsides.

SWEET VIOLETS

BEST VARIETIES

While the flowers of all violets (*Viola*) including pansies (*V.* × *wittrockiana*) and heartsease (*V. tricolor*) are edible, the best flavour comes from sweet violets (*V. odorata*). These keep some of their leaves year-round, but look best in spring. I should warn you that excess consumption of sweet violet flowers can cause nausea and vomiting, while violet roots are even more toxic.

PLANTING

Sweet violets are hardy and will grow in most soils, but prefer to be shaded from the summer's heat and will happily spread under a deciduous tree or fruit bush, for example. Plant potted or plug plants in autumn or early spring, or sow seed in spring.

MAINTENANCE

Deadhead any flowers not used, unless you want them to seed around the garden. Cut dead foliage back to the ground as necessary.

HARVEST

Pick the sweet violet flowers in late winter and early spring and use them judiciously.

BAKE
Flower meringues
(see page 126)

OTHER EDIBLE FLOWERS FOR DECORATION:

All herb flowers
Bergamot (*Monarda didyma*)
Borage (*Borago officinalis*)
Chive (*Allium schoenoprasum*)
Courgette, pumpkin and winter squash
Day lily (*Hemerocallis*)
Nasturtium (*Tropaeolum majus*)
Peas and beans
Pink/carnation (*Dianthus*)
Pot marigold (*Calendula officinalis*)
Primrose (*Primula vulgaris*) and cowslip (*P. veris*)
Violet (*Viola*), pansy (*V.* × *wittrockiana*) and
   particularly heartsease (*Viola tricolor*)

FLOWER MERINGUES

GF WF DF

MAKES ABOUT 50 SMALL MERINGUES

YOU WILL NEED

1–2 × baking sheets, lined with baking paper

INGREDIENTS

Flower syrup:
 50g/2oz caster sugar
 50ml/2fl oz water
 good handful of rose flowers/
  lavender flowers/sweet
  violet flowers/elderflowers/
  lemon verbena leaves/
  scented pelargonium leaves

Meringues:
 1 egg white
 dash of lemon juice
 50ml/2fl oz flower syrup
 gel food colouring (optional)

A bowlful of these petite meringues would make a dainty centrepiece for afternoon tea, especially if scattered with fresh flowers or leaves that correspond to their flavours. Flavour them with edible flowers such as roses, lavender, sweet violets or elderflowers, or leaves from scented pelargonium or lemon verbena plants. Make several differently flavoured batches and swirl with a little food colouring to denote the different flavours.

METHOD

- **For the flower syrup**, put the sugar and water in a small saucepan over a medium heat and stir to dissolve the sugar. Bring to the boil, and simmer for 5 minutes. Take the pan off the heat and add the flowers/leaves, stirring to coat them in syrup and release their natural oils. Leave, covered, to infuse and cool for at least half an hour.
- **For the meringues**, preheat the oven to 120°C/250°F/gas mark ½. Whisk the egg white and lemon juice to soft peaks using a stand mixer or by hand, then, still whisking slowly, trickle in the flower syrup. Once all the syrup is added, continue whisking on high speed until the meringue holds stiff peaks. Spoon into a piping bag and cut the end off to make a hole of around 1cm/½in diameter. Pipe small blobs of about 2cm/¾in diameter on to the baking sheet. To add the food colouring, squeeze a little on to a plate. Drag the point of a skewer (metal or wooden) through the gel, then swirl round the meringue blobs a couple of times, drawing the skewer point upwards as you do so. Make sure you only have a tiny amount of gel on the skewer – large blobs of gel in the meringue will cause the surface to crack and sink. In an electric oven, bake for 30 minutes, then turn the oven down to 50°C/125°F and bake for a further 30 minutes. Turn off the oven but leave the meringues there for at least an hour, preferably overnight. (If you use a gas oven, bake for 40 minutes at gas mark ½, then turn off the oven and leave the meringues in for at least 90 minutes, preferably overnight.)

TO SERVE

Serve in a glass bowl or piled high on a cake stand.

GROW

Elderflowers (see page 125)
Lavender (see page 124)
Lemon verbena (see page 109)
Roses (see page 125)
Scented pelargonium (see page 111)
Sweet violets (see page 125)

LAVENDER SHORTBREAD

MAKES ABOUT 36 BISCUITS

YOU WILL NEED
1 or 2 × baking sheets, lined with baking paper

INGREDIENTS
300g/10oz plain flour
100g/3½oz caster sugar
2 tsp lavender flowers,
    finely chopped or ground
200g/7oz unsalted butter,
    cold and cut into cubes
1 tbsp semi-skimmed milk,
    if needed
1 tsp lavender flowers
1 tsp caster sugar, for dusting

Shortbread is one of the simplest biscuits to make. The key to keeping it short, that is, crumbly and not tough, is not to over-mix the dough or overwork it when rolling out. For a stronger lavender hit, use more lavender flowers or lavender sugar in place of the caster sugar (simply add a teaspoon or two of flowers to a jam jar of sugar, seal, shake and leave to infuse).

GROW
Lavender (see page 124)

METHOD

- Sift the flour and sugar into a large bowl and stir in the lavender flowers. Add the butter and rub it into the mix by hand until it looks like breadcrumbs. Bring together into a single lump of dough, adding milk a drop or two at a time if necessary.
- Wrap in baking paper and chill for 1 hour. Preheat the oven to 170°C/325°F/gas mark 3.
- Roll out the dough on a floured surface to a rectangle about 0.8cm/⅓in thick. Trim the edges, then cut out finger biscuits of 2 × 6cm/¾ × 2½in.
- Transfer the biscuits to the baking sheet(s). Stud 4 lavender flowers in the top of each biscuit.
- Bake for 12–15 minutes until the shortbread is only very lightly coloured. Remove from the oven and transfer to a wire rack. Dust with the sugar and leave to cool.

TO SERVE

Serve as part of an afternoon tea, or for elevenses. This lavender shortbread will keep for up to a month in an airtight tin.

LEFT Lavender flowers are best harvested when still in bud, as pictured here.

BLACKCURRANTS

Blackcurrants surpass even strawberries in the minimum-input, maximum-output stakes. A bush or two planted in the corner of the garden or veg plot will reward you with bowl after bowl of currants year after year.

BEST VARIETIES

Blackcurrant bushes do need a bit of space as they cannot be trained. The most compact variety is 'Ben Sarek'. 'Ben Connan' has large, well-flavoured currants, and, along with other 'Ben' varieties, relatively good disease resistance.

PLANTING

Blackcurrants will grow happily in a little shade, and are tolerant of most soils. Buy bare-root plants from autumn to late winter, or potted plants year-round. Position in the planting hole so that the plant's crown (where the stems and roots join), or the compost level of a potted plant, is around 5cm/2in below soil level. This will encourage new stems to shoot from the base. Allow 1.5m between plants. It is possible to grow blackcurrants permanently in pots of at least 40–50cm/16–20in diameter. 'Ben Sarek' would be the best variety choice for such containerized growing.

MAINTENANCE

Water if it is dry while the fruits are developing, and mulch in spring. In late winter, cut out one-quarter to one-third of the older stems at ground level; aim for an even distribution of the remaining branches around the bush.

HARVEST

Once the fruits have turned fully black, leave for a week or so, then harvest by picking off the entire string at once. It is easier to separate the stalks from the currants once you are in the kitchen.

RIGHT Plant blackcurrants so the crown is below soil level, to encourage new shoots.
FAR RIGHT For full ripeness, leave blackcurrants on the plant for a few days after they have turned a deep purple colour.

BAKE

A muffin for all seasons
(see page 92)
Blackcurrant mini-pavlovas (see page 132)
Chocolate & raspberry bean cake
(see page 68)
Currant friands (see page 123)
Fresh fruit cake (see page 66)
Shades of berry cake
(see page 76)

BLACKCURRANT MINI-PAVLOVAS

MAKES 24 MERINGUES

YOU WILL NEED
1 × baking sheet, lined with baking paper

INGREDIENTS

Meringues:
1 egg white
dash of lemon juice
50g/2oz caster sugar

Decoration:
110ml/4fl oz double cream, whipped
50g/2oz blackcurrants (75 currants)

The blackcurrants on these little meringues look like the buttons on a Pierrot costume. They would be a stylish addition to afternoon tea, or when served as petits fours after dinner.

METHOD
- Preheat the oven to 120°C/225°F/gas mark ½. Whisk the egg white and lemon juice to soft peaks using a stand mixer (or whisking fast by hand), then, still whisking slowly, trickle in the sugar.
- Once all the sugar has been added, continue whisking on high speed until the meringue holds stiff peaks.
- Spoon into a piping bag and cut the end off to make a hole of 1.5cm/⅝in diameter. Pipe lines of meringue, each 5cm/2in long, on to the baking sheet.
- In an electric oven, bake for 30 minutes, then turn the oven down to 50°C/125°F and bake for a further 30 minutes. Turn off the oven but leave the meringues there for at least an hour, preferably overnight. (If you use a gas oven, bake for 40 minutes at gas mark ½, then turn off the oven and leave the meringues in for at least 90 minutes, preferably overnight.)

TO SERVE
Pipe a line of the whipped cream along the top of each meringue and top each one with three blackcurrants.

GROW
Blackcurrants
(see page 130)

PUDDINGS

APPLES

Apples are a long-term investment in the garden, but they are well worth the wait. Much of the fruit sold in the shops is imported from the other side of the world, or stored for months, or both, and inevitably some of the natural sugars are lost. Plus, by growing your own, you can choose from the hundreds of varieties available. Apple trees do not require a lot of space, and they grow just as happily in a pot or when planted in the garden against a fence.

BEST VARIETIES

When choosing varieties, consider whether you want the fruit to cook down into a purée or to hold its form. Cooking apples that break down include 'Bramley's Seedling' and the compact 'Emneth Early', whereas 'Blenheim Orange' will hold its shape. Dessert apples tend to be sweeter and can be grated before they are cooked, or else baked in recipes requiring apples that keep their shape. Good choices are 'Egremont Russet', 'Falstaff' and 'Cox's Orange Pippin'.

PLANTING

Plant trees (whether growing in pots or bare-root) from autumn to spring. First put in wires to train them on, or stake free-standing trees. An open, sunny aspect is best, and the trees will tolerate most soils. How far apart your trees need to be spaced depends on if/how each is trained and on to which rootstock it is grafted. Dwarfed cordons can be planted as little as 75cm/30in apart, while large trees should be up to 9m/30ft apart.

MAINTENANCE

Water in dry spells, especially once the tree is flowering and then producing fruit. An annual mulch in spring will help conserve moisture. The tree's own 'June drop' usually disposes of excess young fruits, but remove most of any large clusters to allow decent-sized apples to develop. Prune annually, in summer (for trained trees) or winter (for free-standing ones), cutting branches back to 2–3 buds above last year's cut; see page 171 for where to find pruning advice.

HARVEST

An apple is ready to harvest if its stalk breaks naturally when the fruit is gently lifted from the branch. Depending on the variety this can be from late summer to early winter.

ABOVE Lemon juice will prevent peeled and cut apples from browning.
RIGHT Apples are ready to harvest when the stalk breaks easily from the branch.

BAKE

A muffin for all seasons (see page 92)
Apple pie (see page 138)
Mince pies (see page 98)
Toffee apple cupcakes (see page 96)

GROW
Apples (see page 136)
Lemons
(see page 119)

APPLE PIE

SERVES 10

YOU WILL NEED

1 × baking sheet
1 × deep pie dish, 24–25cm/
    9½–10in diameter, greased

INGREDIENTS

Pastry case:
    350g/12oz plain flour
    125g/4oz unsalted butter, chilled
    125g/4oz light muscovado sugar
    2 eggs, beaten

Filling:
    1 tbsp cornflour
    2 tbsp (golden) caster sugar
    6 dessert apples that keep
        their form
    2 large cooking apples that
        break down
    ½ lemon, juice

Topping:
    1 egg, beaten with a small
        pinch of salt
    1 tsp ground cinnamon
    1 tbsp demerara sugar

The choice of apple in your pie is a matter of taste and texture. Do you want definite pieces of apple or a general blend (I hesitate to say mush, but that is essentially what it is)? This recipe is the best of both worlds – the apples are completely enclosed with rich buttery pastry and dusted with cinnamon sugar.

METHOD

- **For the pastry case**, roll out two-thirds of the pastry so that it is big enough to line the dish, and transfer it carefully. Remove the overhang and use it to cut out leaves or other shapes to decorate the top of the pie. Roll out the remaining one-third to create a disc big enough to form the pie lid, remembering the apples will be mounded up in the dish; then return the lid to the refrigerator on a sheet of baking paper. Preheat the oven to 190°C/375°F/gas mark 5 and place the baking sheet on the middle shelf.
- **For the filling**, mix the cornflour and caster sugar together in a small bowl. Peel, core and slice the apples, and arrange in the dish in alternate tiers of the two varieties. Sprinkle each tier with lemon juice and a heaped teaspoon of the cornflour/sugar mix. Mound the final tiers towards the centre of the dish slightly.
- **For the topping**, brush the edge of the pastry base with the egg and lay the lid over the top, cutting off any excess and pressing the edges together with a fork to seal them. Brush the lid with beaten egg, lay on the decorative leaves, brush them with egg and cut a small steam hole in the centre of the lid. Mix the cinnamon and demerara sugar in a bowl and sprinkle it over the pie top. Put the dish on the baking sheet in the oven. Bake for 30–40 minutes, until the pastry is hard when tapped and the apples soft. (The cinnamon and brown sugar in the pastry make it appear darker than usual.) Remove from the oven and leave to settle for a bit.

TO SERVE

Serve hot, but not straight from the oven, with lashings of cream.

PLUMS

Fat, sweet, juicy plums herald the beginning of the end of summer, the most bounteous time of year in the kitchen garden. If you leave the fruits to ripen on the tree until it takes only a look to make them fall into your hand, you will be rewarded with the best plums you have ever tasted.

BEST VARIETIES

Plum varieties are split into culinary and dessert plums, but to be honest even the former varieties are delicious to eat raw when compared with a supermarket fruit. Good choices are 'Czar', and the reliable 'Opal' and 'Victoria', or try a greengage instead such as 'Cambridge Gage'. All of these are self-fertile, so you need only one tree for successful fertilization. Damsons, a type of plum, are best cooked and have a much more intense flavour, which is ideal for jams or mincemeat (see page 98).

PLANTING

Plums prefer a sunny site with shelter from wind, and are ideal for training against a sunny wall or fence (a fan shape is the traditional form, but they can also be grown in cordons). They can be grown in large pots too. Plant bare-root trees in autumn or late winter, and potted trees in autumn or spring, staking or tying them to wires. Cordons should be planted 75cm/30in apart, fans will need 4–5m/13–16ft between trees and free-standing plums on semi-dwarfing rootstocks should be set 2.5–3.5m/8–12ft apart.

MAINTENANCE

Unlike other tree fruit, plums are pruned when in leaf, to avoid spreading a couple of specific plum diseases. An annual prune in spring (for bush trees) or summer (for trained ones) is all that is required (see pages 21–2). Make sure no fruit is left rotting on the tree, and mulch it with organic matter in spring.

HARVEST

Depending on the variety, plums will ripen from midsummer to autumn. If possible leave the fruit on the tree until the merest nudge knocks it off the branch, but, if the cold weather is imminent or wasps are a nuisance, pick the fruit when unripe and leave it to develop indoors.

BAKE
Mince pies (see page 98)
Roasted plum cheesecake
(see facing page)

RIGHT Leave plums to ripen for as long as possible on the tree.

ROASTED PLUM CHEESECAKE

SERVES 8–10

YOU WILL NEED

1 × spring-form, round cake tin, 23cm/9in diameter, greased and base-lined

1 × brownie or small roasting tin, 20 × 25 × 3cm/ 8 × 10 × 1¼in

INGREDIENTS

Roasted plums:

750–800g/1lb 10oz–1lb 12oz plums, halved and pitted

75g/2½oz caster sugar

150ml/¼ pint water

Base:

200g/7oz ginger biscuits

100g/3½oz unsalted butter

Cheesecake:

300g/10oz mascarpone

300g/10oz crème fraîche

1 tsp vanilla extract

4 tbsp icing sugar

GROW
Plums
(see facing page)

This delightful, light pudding for late summer is perfect for that last evening meal of the year under the stars. Before you roast the plums always check that you have enough halves to cover the base completely, cut side down, with at least two whole plums/four halves left over. The components of this plum cheesecake can be made in advance and assembled on the day.

METHOD

- **For the roasted plums**, preheat the oven to 170°C/325°F/gas mark 3. Put the plums, sugar and water in the roasting tin (so that the fruit fits snugly in one layer). Bake for 30 minutes until soft, then remove from the oven, drain and cool.
- **For the base**, bash (or whizz in a food processor) the biscuits to crumbs. Melt the butter. Combine the crumbs and butter until they are fully coated, then press into the base of the lined spring-form tin (use a potato masher). Chill for at least half an hour. Then arrange the plum halves, cut side down, over the base to cover it completely. Return the base to the refrigerator. Push the remaining plums through a sieve to make a purée, and put a large spoonful into a piping bag, and set aside.
- **For the cheesecake**, whisk together the cheesecake ingredients. Put about one-third of it into a separate bowl. Whisk the remaining plum purée into the remaining cheesecake mix, to taste, then spread it over the plum base. Chill for 10 minutes, then top with the plain cheesecake from the separate bowl, and level. Pipe blobs of plum purée around the edge, and another circle within that. Pull a skewer or knife through each blob to feather it. Chill for 3 hours before serving.

TO SERVE

Serve chilled, on the day of making.

FRUITY PIZZA

MAKES 8 SMALL PIZZAS

YOU WILL NEED
1 × pizza stone or a baking sheet
1 × baking sheet, floured

INGREDIENTS

Dough:
250g/8oz strong white
   bread flour
250g/8oz plain flour
1½ tsp fast-action dried yeast
1 tsp salt
1 tsp caster sugar
320ml/11fl oz warm water
   (100ml/3½fl oz boiling
   water, the rest cold water)
1 tbsp olive oil

**TOPPING SUGGESTIONS
(QUANTITIES FOR ONE PIZZA):**

Berries and currants topping:
75g/2½oz raspberries,
   strawberries, red- or
   blackcurrants and/or
   blueberries, or a mixture of
   some or all of these
2 tbsp jam

Apple or pear topping:
1 tsp muscovado sugar
small knob of butter
½ apple or pear, thinly sliced

Fig and almond topping:
2–3 figs
runny honey, for drizzling
1–2 tbsp flaked almonds

Cinnamon plum topping:
½ tsp ground cinnamon
1–2 plums, pitted and
   thinly sliced
½ tsp demarara sugar

These pizzas are a great finish to a meal of their savoury counterparts, and a good way to involve children with the cooking. Some suggested toppings are given below, but get creative and make up your own.

METHOD

- **For the dough**, sift all the dry ingredients together, and pour in the water and oil. Mix to a dough and knead until it is soft and silky (about 10 minutes in a stand mixer with a dough hook). Cover and leave in a warm place to double in size. Preheat the oven to as hot as it will go (or fire up the pizza oven, if you are lucky enough to have one), but to at least 220°C/425°F/gas mark 7; place a pizza stone or baking sheet inside to warm up. Divide the dough into 8 pieces and roll out each to about the size of a side plate. Put a couple on the floured baking sheet, then add the toppings.
- **For the berry and currant topping**, spread the jam on the dough, then top with the berries and currants. Once it is out of the oven, you could add a couple of squares of chocolate, roughly chopped. Alternatively omit the jam and add blobs of Lemon curd (see page 121) to the cooked pizza.
- **For the apple or pear topping**, mash the sugar into the butter with a fork and spread over the dough. Lay over the apple or pear slices.
- **For the fig and almond topping**, cut each fig into one-eighths and put on the dough. Drizzle with honey and scatter with flaked almonds.
- **For the cinnamon plum topping**, dust the dough with cinnamon. Lay the plum slices over the dough and scatter with the sugar.

TO SERVE

Slide the pizzas off the baking sheet on to the preheated stone/baking sheet and cook for 7–10 minutes, until the bases are crisp and the crusts slightly browned. Remove from the oven and repeat to bake the other pizzas. Serve hot, sliced into wedges, with more honey/jam/melted chocolate, as appropriate, for drizzling over the top.

GROW
Apples (see page 136)
Berries (see pages 64, 74 and 106)
Currants (see pages 122 and 130)
Figs (see page 150)
Lemons (see page 119)
Pears (see page 146)
Plums (see page 140)

CHILLIES

BAKE
Chilli chocolate mudcake
(see page 144)

Chillies are an increasingly popular crop for the home-grower, not least because cultivating your own from seed allows for a far, far greater range of heat levels and flavours than the choice on a supermarket shelf would indicate was possible.

BEST VARIETIES

Consider how spicy you like your chillies before choosing which varieties to grow. The fruitiest flavours come from the habanero types (also known as Scotch bonnet chillies), which range from the mild 'Apricot' through quite spicy 'Hot Scotch' and very hot 'Submarine' to the eye-watering 'Devil's Rib'. Chillies can also be very pretty plants to grow: the multicoloured 'Numex Twilight' is a great example, while 'Spike' would be a good choice for the sugar glass (see page 145).

PLANTING

Sow chillies in late winter, indoors and preferably in a heated propagator as they need temperatures of 18°C/65°F+ to germinate. Alternatively buy young plants from garden centres or specialist growers. Once there is little risk of frosts plant out into the sunniest, hottest patch of ground you have, or set in a pot and position it on a patio or windowsill. Space plants 40cm/16in apart.

MAINTENANCE

If the branches of large-fruited varieties – and even smaller-fruited ones – get overladen, tie them to a stake, using the three-loop method (see page 26). Keep plants well-watered and fed, especially those in pots. Plants grown under cover will benefit from being sprayed with water when they are flowering, to help pollination.

HARVEST

Chillies will be ready to harvest from midsummer, depending on the variety and when they were sown. A chilli is mature when it feels firm to the touch, and can be picked then, even if it is green. For the best flavour wait until the chilli is ripe, when it has developed its final colouring.

RIGHT Chillies, here on the variety 'Spike', once mature can be picked green or red.

GROW

Chillies (see page 143)
Pumpkins &
winter squashes
(see page 84)

CHILLI CHOCOLATE MUDCAKE

MAKES A SINGLE-LAYER CAKE

YOU WILL NEED

- 1 × spring-form, round cake tin, 23cm/9in diameter, greased and base-lined
- 1 × small square/rectangular roasting/oven tray (one side at least c.20cm/8in long), lined with oil-coated foil (making sure the foil comes a couple of centimetres up the sides)
- 1 × sugar or infra-red thermometer

INGREDIENTS

Cake:
- 2 red chillies
- 250g/8½oz plain dark chocolate (70 per cent cocoa solids), coarsely chopped
- 250g/8½oz unsalted butter, diced
- 4 eggs
- 200g/7oz muscovado sugar
- 100g/3½oz grated pumpkin or butternut squash
- 100g/3½oz plain flour
- 1 tsp baking powder
- pinch of salt

Ganache:
- 1 red chilli
- 300ml/½ pint double cream
- 1 tbsp caster sugar
- 250g/8½oz plain dark chocolate (70 per cent cocoa solids), finely chopped
- 50g/2oz unsalted butter

Sugar glass shards:
- 4–6 small red chillies
- 180g/6oz granulated sugar
- 65ml/2fl oz liquid glucose
- 125ml/4fl oz water
- red food colouring

Adding chilli takes the humble mudcake to another level, and makes this an altogether sophisticated dessert. The longer the cake is left, the fudgier the texture becomes, so bake it the day before serving if possible, but beware – the chilli heat also develops over time! The sugar glass shards can also be prepared in advance and stored in an airtight tin.

METHOD

- **For the cake**, first blacken the skins of the chillies under the grill, then seal them, while still hot, in a plastic bag and leave to cool. Once cool, peel off the skins, take out the seeds and finely chop the flesh. Preheat the oven to 170°C/325°F/gas mark 3. Melt the chocolate and prepared chilli in a bowl set over a pan of simmering water, then remove from the heat. Add the butter and stir until melted and smooth. Separate the eggs and whisk the egg whites until they form soft peaks; set aside. Beat the egg yolks and sugar together until creamy, then stir in the melted chilli chocolate mix, followed by the pumpkin and finally the flour, baking powder and salt. Stir through a spoonful of the egg white, then carefully fold in the rest until fully incorporated. Bake for 30 minutes, taking it out when there is still a slight tremor in the middle of the cake when wobbled. Leave to cool for 10 minutes in the tin before turning out on to a wire rack to cool completely.
- **For the ganache**, cut the chilli in half and put into a saucepan with the cream and sugar. Leave to infuse for at least two hours, then bring to a boil over a medium heat, stirring to make sure the sugar is fully dissolved. Put the chocolate in a large bowl and pour over half of the cream (through a sieve to catch the chilli and any loose seeds). Stir to melt the chocolate, then pour over the remaining cream, add the butter and continue stirring until the mix is smooth and glossy. Allow to cool slightly before pouring/spreading over the cake.
- **For the sugar glass shards**, put the remaining ingredients in a saucepan and bring to the boil, stirring all the time. Once the glazing liquid reaches 150°C/300°F (or 'hard crack'), take it off the heat and allow it to cool to 130°C/250°F, when it should be poured immediately on to the prepared baking sheet. Very quickly, position the chillies on the glazing liquid. Once completely cool, score the glass sheet with a sharp knife to mark where you would like it to break (this helps, but does not always work), then with one strong, swift blow, strike the middle of the sheet with a hammer or similar tool. Stick the resultant shards into the ganache-covered cake.

TO SERVE

Serve with a scoop of cooling vanilla ice cream.

PEARS

Whenever I see pears in the supermarket I am reminded of an Eddie Izzard sketch in which he mimes using the fruit to hammer in nails, because it is so unripe. If you grow your own, you will never have to wait weeks for pears to ripen in the fruit bowl again.

BAKE
Mince pies (see page 98)
Upside-down pear cake
(see facing page)

BEST VARIETIES

There is a reason that 'Conference' pears are so widely available – this variety is reliable and has a good flavour, but 'Buerré Bosc' (or simply 'Bosc') is the better for baking. 'Concorde' has a compact growth habit. Choose varieties from the same pollination group and on a suitable rootstock – dwarfing, or whatever – for your situation.

PLANTING

Plant trees (available in pots or bare-root) from autumn to spring. At the same time fix wires to train them on, or stake free-standing trees. Early pear blossom can be damaged by spring winds and frosts, so plant in a sheltered, warm spot. Cordons should be placed 75cm/30in apart; leave at least 2.5m/8ft between full-sized trees, depending on their rootstock. Pears can also be grown permanently in large pots, but be sure to choose a tree on a dwarfing rootstock.

MAINTENANCE

Water in dry spells, especially once the tree is flowering and producing fruit. Remove most of the fruitlets of any large clusters to allow a few decent-sized pears to develop. Prune annually, in summer (for trained trees) or in winter (for free-standing ones); see page 171 for where to obtain pruning advice.

HARVEST

Pears are ready to harvest when the stalk breaks naturally from the branch when the fruit is gently lifted. Depending on the variety this can be from late summer to mid-autumn. The flesh should be sweet but not starchy, and they will still need a little ripening indoors.

BELOW Pears will still need a little ripening once picked, but not as long as shop-bought fruit.

UPSIDE-DOWN PEAR CAKE

MAKES A SINGLE-LAYER CAKE

YOU WILL NEED

1 × deep, round cake tin, 20cm/8in diameter; line the base of a loose-bottomed tin if it has a silicone seal, otherwise fully line the tin

INGREDIENTS

Caramel pears base:
100g/3½oz caster
    or granulated sugar
15g/½oz unsalted butter
4–5 pears

Sponge:
200g/7oz peeled and
    cored pears
2 tsp vanilla extract
200g/7oz plain flour
50g/2oz ground almonds
2½ tsp baking powder
¼ tsp salt
120g/4oz unsalted butter
100g/3½oz light
    muscovado sugar
2 eggs

This sticky, caramel pear cake is just the thing for a cold winter's night. It is also quite accommodating for a dinner party schedule, as it is best served warm rather than hot, so that the delicate flavour of the pears really comes through.

METHOD

- **For the caramel pears base**, pour the sugar into a saucepan so that it covers the base in an even tier and put over a medium heat. Only when the sugar has almost all melted should you stir the contents until it is a uniform, golden brown liquid. Take the pan off the heat, stir in the butter until it has melted, then pour into the prepared tin to cover the base evenly. Leave to cool. Preheat the oven to 180°C/350°F/gas mark 4. Peel, core and halve the pears and lay cut side down on the caramel, top end inwards so that they form a nice circular pattern and cover the base of the tin.
- **For the sponge**, blend the pears and vanilla extract into a purée, using a stick blender if possible, and set aside. Mix the flour with the ground almonds, baking powder and salt and set aside. Cream the butter and sugar together, then beat in the eggs, followed by the puréed pears. Finally sift in the dry ingredients and beat until incorporated. Pour the mixture into the tin and spread over the pears, levelling off the top. Bake for 45–55 minutes, until a skewer comes out clean, then remove from the oven and leave to cool in the tin for 15 minutes.

TO SERVE

Turn out on to a serving plate (leave to cool further if necessary) and peel off the baking paper. Serve warm, perhaps with a drizzle of cream.

GROW
Pears (see facing page)

GROW
Mint (see page 110)
Strawberries
(see page 106)

STRAWBERRY TART

SERVES 8–10

YOU WILL NEED

1 × flan tin, 23–25cm/9–10in diameter, greased

INGREDIENTS

Pastry case:

230g/8oz plain flour
80g/2½oz unsalted butter, chilled
80g/2½oz caster sugar
2 eggs
pinch of salt

Crème pâtissière:

1 vanilla pod
500ml/17½fl oz milk
6 egg yolks
120g/4oz caster sugar
2 tbsp cornflour

Filling:

600–800g/1lb 4oz–1lb 12oz strawberries
mint sprigs/leaves (optional)

Decoration:

100g/3½oz apricot jam
OR icing sugar, for dusting

This tart is perfect for a summer's dinner party. It looks so impressive that your guests will think you have bought it, and your delicious sun-ripened strawberries will be the star of the show. The components can be prepared in advance and assembled at the last minute.

METHOD

- **For the pastry case**, blind bake the case and leave to cool.
- **For the crème pâtissière**, slice the vanilla pod in half along its length. Using the back of the knife, scrape out the tiny black seeds within. Put the seeds and pod with the milk in a large, heavy-based saucepan over a medium heat. Bring the milk to the boil, then take the pan off the heat and leave to infuse for 10 minutes. Meanwhile whisk the egg yolks into the sugar and cornflour in a large bowl until the mix is smooth but not pale. Bring the milk back to the boil, and pour one-third to one-half of it into the egg mixture, whisking as you pour. Add in the remaining milk, whisk it to a smooth mixture, then pour it all through a sieve back into the saucepan. Bring to the boil and simmer for 1 minute, whisking the whole time, then take off the heat. The crème pâtissière should feel smooth and thick. Pour it into a bowl and lay a piece of baking paper over the surface, to prevent a skin forming. Leave the crème pâtissière to cool, then store it in the refrigerator until you are ready to assemble the tart.
- **For the filling**, spread the crème pâtissière in the pastry case. Slice the tops off the strawberries and arrange as closely together as possible, cut side down, in the tart. Dot a few sprigs of mint around the strawberries, if using.

TO SERVE

For the patisserie look, gently heat the apricot jam over a low heat to loosen it, then brush over the whole tart to glaze. Alternatively dust with icing sugar just before serving.

FIGS

Soft, luscious figs speak of lazy days in the sunshine and decadent feasts. They are easy to grow, and will quickly spread to cover a wall or fill a sunny spot. Their architectural foliage looks as good as the figs taste.

BEST VARIETIES

It is hard to beat 'Brown Turkey' for availability and reliable crops in cool-temperate climates, but in warmer ones or in a greenhouse 'Rouge de Bordeaux' and 'Osborn's Prolific' are better for flavour.

PLANTING

In order to fruit well, figs must be in a sheltered, warm and light spot; training against a wall or planting in a pot on a sunny patio are the best options. In cool-temperate climates, they will need protection from frosts and cold weather, either by moving the pot under cover or by covering the plant with fleece.

Fig trees are sold in pots. Plant in the spring, after the last frost. To encourage the plant to fruit rather than put on lots of foliage, it is best to restrict the roots. Growing in a container is therefore ideal, but make sure you will still be able to move it into shelter if necessary. Otherwise figs are an ideal crop for a narrow border along a wall; make a planting pit roughly 60cm/24in square and line the sides with paving slabs or similar. A tree trained in a fan against a wall will need a space 3.5m/12ft wide and 2.5m/8ft high.

MAINTENANCE

Where fig roots have been restricted by a pit or container, provide regular watering and feeding through spring and summer. In winter figs need less water and no fertilizer, but do not let the compost dry out completely. Repot figs grown in containers every couple of years, even if each is put back into the same pot with fresh compost. Prune in spring (see pages 21–2).

RIGHT The skin colour of ripe figs will depend on the variety.

HARVEST

Figs are ready to pick when the skin is beginning to split, the fruit is soft and hanging down off the branch. The skin colour depends on the variety. Hold on to the stalk and snap the fruit off the branch.

BAKE
Fig tart
(see facing page)

FIG TART

SERVES 12

YOU WILL NEED
1 × loose-bottomed, metal flan tin, 20 × 30cm/
   8 × 12in, greased
1 × baking sheet

INGREDIENTS

Pastry case:
   200g/7oz plain flour
   60g/2oz ground almonds
   70g/2½oz unsalted butter, chilled
   70g/2½oz caster sugar
   2 eggs, beaten

Filling:
   25g/1oz unsalted butter
   3 eggs
   100g/3½oz caster sugar
   25g/1oz ground almonds
   1 tbsp plain flour
   150ml/¼ pint double cream
   1 tbsp amaretto liqueur (optional)
   6 fresh figs, halved lengthways

METHOD

- **For the pastry case**, preheat the oven to 180°C/350°F/gas mark 4, and put the baking sheet on the middle shelf. Roll out the pastry and line the tin. Trim off the excess so the edges are flush with the tin and put it into the refrigerator while you make the filling.
- **For the filling**, melt the butter. Beat the eggs, sugar, almonds and flour together, then whisk in the butter, cream and amaretto for 1–2 minutes until smooth (this is best done using a stand mixer if possible). Arrange the figs in the pastry case, cut side up (little blobs of pastry under the figs can help to keep the tops level). Then put the tart on to the baking sheet in the oven. Pour in the custard, trying not to cover the tops of the figs. (Pouring the custard once the tart is on the oven shelf minimizes the risk of spillages.) Bake for 30–40 minutes, or until the custard has set.

TO SERVE

Serve warm.

This impressive tart is very simple to make. The figs are merely halved, maximizing the contrast between their sumptuous purple flesh and the sunshine yellow custard filling, and showing them off to their best advantage.

GROW
Figs (see facing page)

HAZELNUTS

BAKE
Hazelnut & rosemary
pavlova
(see facing page)

Cobnuts (*Corylus avellana*) and filberts (*C. maxima*) are the
names given to hazelnuts when they are in cultivation, the main
difference being that cobnuts have a shorter husk enclosing the nut.
These deciduous shrubs require a bit of space, but are relatively low
maintenance, and the pruned branches can also usefully supply your
garden with bean poles and stakes.

BEST VARIETIES

Unless there is hazel growing in the immediate
surrounding area, you need two plants to get
decent wind pollination, and therefore nuts.
Cobnut varieties include 'Cosford Cob' and
'Pearson's Prolific', and good-flavoured filberts
are 'Kentish Cob' and 'Gunslebert'.

PLANTING

A sunny spot is best; hazel will grow, but may
not fruit well, in shade. Buy bare-root or potted
plants, and plant in autumn, winter (for bare-
root) or spring. Set them 5m/16ft apart, unless
you are creating a hedge, in which case 3m/10ft
between plants is enough. It is fine to grow your
hazels as they would in the wild, that is, with all
the stems originating from the base. However it
is possible to train them on a 'leg', a single stem/
trunk of 30–45cm/12–18in, with all the branches
then sprouting off the top of that. If you opt for
this method, stake the tree until it is established.

MAINTENANCE

Keep the plants watered during dry spells, and
mulch in spring. The easiest way to prune is to
remove one-quarter to one-third of the stems at
the base (or at the top of the leg) in late winter
or early spring, as this will also supply you with
bean poles for the year. In summer remove any
suckers (small branches) that try to grow around
the base of the leg.

HARVEST

Hazelnuts will be ready in autumn, when the
husks start to yellow. Do not leave them too
long, or the squirrels will take your entire crop;
but do not pick them too early either. Spread
the nuts in a single layer in boxes lined with
newspaper in a cool, dry place and leave for a few
weeks. Remove the husks from dried nuts and
store in a dry place with good air circulation (e.g.
in a net bag, not a sealed box).

RIGHT The brown skins of hazelnuts can be rubbed
off before grinding.

HAZELNUT & ROSEMARY PAVLOVA

GF WF

MAKES ONE LARGE PAVLOVA

YOU WILL NEED

1 × baking sheet (preferably square rather than rectangular), at least 30 × 30cm (12 × 12in), lined with baking paper

INGREDIENTS

Ground hazelnuts:
85g/3oz hazelnuts, toasted

Meringue:
3 egg whites
dash of lemon juice
150g/5oz caster sugar

Filling/topping:
250ml/9fl oz double cream, whipped
2 sprigs of rosemary, finely chopped, plus more sprigs for decoration
50g/2oz toasted hazelnuts, roughly chopped
plain dark chocolate shavings

Baking with nuts need not mean a dense, heavy cake. Here hazelnuts are used, with accents of rosemary and chocolate, to create a sophisticated pavlova.

METHOD

- **For the ground hazelnuts**, rub the hazelnuts between your hands or two tea towels to remove the dark outer skins, then chop them in a food processor until finely ground. Weigh out 75g/2½oz and set aside.
- **For the meringue**, preheat the oven to 150°C/300°F/ gas mark 2. Whisk the egg whites and lemon juice to soft peaks using a stand mixer (or whisk fast by hand), then, still whisking slowly, trickle in the sugar. Once it has all been incorporated, continue whisking quickly until the meringue forms stiff peaks. Fold in the ground hazelnuts until they are well dispersed through the meringue. Use two-thirds of the meringue to make a large disc (20–25cm/8–10in diameter) on the baking sheet. Spoon the remaining meringue into a piping bag and add peaked meringue blobs all around the edge of the disc; spread any leftovers in the middle. Bake for 1 hour, then turn off the oven and leave the meringue there for at least another hour, preferably overnight.

TO ASSEMBLE

Spread the cream over the middle of the pavlova base, then scatter over the chopped rosemary and nuts and the chocolate shavings. Finish with a few sprigs of rosemary.

GROW
Hazelnuts
(see facing page)
Rosemary
(see page 110)

SAVOURY BAKES

POPPIES

It is true that the aesthetic appeal of some vegetables is limited, but the all-too-brief beauty of the poppy flower cannot be denied. The flowers can be enjoyed for their full life too, as it is the seeds that are the aim here. Leave a seed head or two standing – the birds will appreciate it, and you will probably get some self-sown flowers next year too.

BEST VARIETIES

Seeds of the red field or Flanders poppy (*Papaver rhoeas*) and the pale purple opium poppy (*P. somniferum*) are suitable to cook with. In some countries it is illegal to grow opium poppies without a licence, while in other countries it is acceptable to grow them (just not to process the seeds into opium!) so please check your garden is operating within the law.

PLANTING

In spring or autumn sow seeds direct into well-drained soil or a pot in a sunny position. It is possible to buy plug plants, but results may not be as good, because poppy seedlings do not appreciate disturbance. Space plants 10cm/4in (*P. rhoeas*) or 25cm/10in (*P. somniferum*) apart.

MAINTENANCE

Just enjoy the flowers.

HARVEST

Only the seeds can be eaten – all other parts of poppies are toxic. Once the petals fall away to reveal the seed head in late summer/autumn, wait for it to dry out a bit. The seeds will be ripe when the seed head can be shaken like a rattle. Cut the seed head off the stalk, and extract the seeds into a paper bag. Leave the sealed bag in a dry place for a couple of weeks until the seeds are completely dry, then pour into a jar to store until needed. If you are uncertain when the seed head may be ripe and do not want to miss your seed collection opportunity, tie a paper bag over the top of the stalk. The seed head will ripen within the bag, and any loose seeds are collected within it.

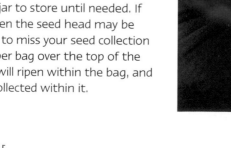

BAKE
Poppy seed flower-pot bread (see facing page)

BELOW The common field (or Flanders) poppy, *Papaver rhoeas*, flowers only briefly.

POPPY SEED FLOWER-POT BREAD

DF

MAKES 6 ROLLS

YOU WILL NEED

6 small prepared clay flower pots, the base and
sides lined with baking paper
1 × baking sheet

INGREDIENTS

Pot preparation:
2 tbsp olive oil

Bread:
1kg/1lb 3oz bread or strong flour
2 tsp fast-action dried yeast
600ml/1 pint warm water (200ml/7fl oz
boiling water, the remainder cold water)
1 tbsp olive oil
3 tsp salt
3 tsp poppy seeds

Decoration:
olive oil, for glazing
½ tsp poppy seeds, for sprinkling

These little seeded
rolls are baked in
real clay flower pots,
and can be returned
to the pots for serving. It is probably best to
purchase new pots; keep them to a diameter
and height less than 15cm/6in and ideally to
around 9cm/3½in. White bread flour shows off
the poppy seeds to best advantage, but could be
substituted in whole or part with wholemeal or
granary flour.

GROW
Poppies
(see facing page)

METHOD

- **To prepare the pots**, wash them thoroughly and
  allow to dry. Preheat the oven to 180°C/350°F/gas
  mark 4. Brush the insides of the pots liberally with
  the olive oil and put the pots on the baking sheet.
  Bake for an hour, allow to cool, then wash and
  dry again. (Such preparation needs to be done
  only once.)

- **For the bread**, sift the flour into a large mixing
  bowl and stir in the yeast. Pour in the warm
  water, then the olive oil. Mix for 5 minutes
  before adding the salt and poppy seeds. Knead
  until the dough is smooth and elastic. Divide
  the dough into 6 equal pieces (unless your
  pots are of different sizes, in which case split it
  up appropriately) and put into the lined pots,
  pressing into a rough pot shape to fit. Cover with
  clingfilm and leave in a warm place for an hour
  until the dough has doubled in size. Meanwhile
  preheat the oven to 200°C/400°F/gas mark 6.
  Remove the clingfilm, and put the pots on to
  the baking sheet. Brush the tops with olive oil
  and sprinkle with poppy seeds. Bake for around
  30 minutes; the rolls should sound hollow when
  tapped on the base. Remove from the oven, turn
  the rolls out of the pots and put them on to a
  wire rack to cool.

TO SERVE

Serve warm or cold, in the pots, perhaps as part of a
ploughman's (or gardener's) lunch.

PEAS

Eating peas straight from the pod, direct from the plant, is one of the home-grower's greatest pleasures, and a considerable temptation when working in the garden. If you can get them to the kitchen, cook them as soon as possible after picking, to retain that super-sweet flavour. If not, well, the shoots and flowers are just as tasty!

BEST VARIETIES

To ensure a good supply over spring and summer, plant early, second early and maincrop varieties in succession. The sweetest varieties are the petit-pois types. Good choices are 'Kelvedon Wonder' (early), 'Early Onward' (second early) and 'Balmoral' (maincrop). Any culinary pea flower or shoot is edible, but to grow plants just for the shoots choose 'Twinkle' (early).

PLANTING

Peas like an open, sunny spot, in a soil enriched with plenty of organic matter. Sow in autumn/ winter or spring; even with a single variety it is a good idea to sow at regular intervals. Seeds can be sown in lengths of guttering, and then the whole thing – plants, compost and all – can be slid into a prepared drill when the seedlings are established. Plants can be set as close as 5cm/2in apart, with the rows as far apart as the plants will be high (check the seed packet). Peas also do well in pots, but choose dwarf varieties for this, as these will not need staking.

MAINTENANCE

Protect peas from marauding mice and birds, especially pigeons. Most peas (not the dwarf varieties) will need supports to climb up. Either put in a row of twiggy sticks alongside the seedlings, or stretch some netting between posts at either end of the row. The peas will cling on to the support themselves; they will not need tying in.

HARVEST

Pick the flowers, shoots and pods whenever they are ready. Regular picking of the pods will encourage the development of more flowers and pods.

BAKE
Pea cheesecake
(see page 160)

ABOVE Support young pea plants with twiggy sticks.
RIGHT Pea flowers are delicious, but leave some to develop into pods of peas.

PEA CHEESECAKE

SERVES
4–6 AS A LIGHT LUNCH
WITH SALAD
8–10 AS A STARTER

YOU WILL NEED
1 × spring-form, round cake tin,
23cm/9in diameter, greased and
base-lined

INGREDIENTS

Base tier:
200g/7oz oatcakes
100g/3½oz unsalted butter

Parmesan crisps:
20g/¾oz Parmesan cheese,
finely grated

Pea purée:
100g/3½oz butter
2 garlic cloves, crushed
300g/10oz peas

Filling:
360g/12oz cream cheese
120ml/4fl oz double cream
4 eggs
1 lemon, zest
salt and pepper, to taste
100g/3½oz peas

Decoration:
handful of pea shoots
edible flowers (for example,
pea flowers, violas)

This unusual dish is a delicious light lunch or summer
starter, and uses everything but the pod itself from the
pea plant. (If you want to save your pea flowers to turn
into more peas, omit them or use other edible flowers.)
Savoury cheesecakes are a great alternative to quiches and
tarts; and as this recipe uses oatcakes for the base it is
wheat-free too.

METHOD

- **For the base tier**, put the oatcakes in a food bag and bash
  with a rolling pin until they are reduced to crumbs. Melt the
  butter, then combine with the crumbs in a bowl, mixing
  so they are all coated. Press into the base of the tin in an
  even tier (a potato masher is the best tool here). Chill in the
  refrigerator for at least half an hour.
- **For the Parmesan crisps**, preheat the oven to 180°C/350°F/
  gas mark 4. Put 10 large pinches of grated cheese on to a
  baking sheet, leaving space for them to spread. Place the
  baking sheet in the oven and, watching all the time, leave the
  cheese to melt into flat, slightly browned crisps. Remove from
  the oven and cool the crisps on the baking sheet.
- **For the pea purée**, melt the butter in a frying pan. Add
  the garlic to the butter as it melts, but do not let the garlic
  brown. Pour over the peas and blend to a rough purée.
- **For the filling**, whisk the cream cheese, double cream, eggs
  and lemon zest together in a large bowl. Add the pea purée,
  season with salt and pepper and whisk again until everything
  is incorporated. Stir in the whole peas. Pour the filling over
  the base tier and bake for 35–40 minutes until the cheesecake
  does not wobble when the tin is shaken, and the top is
  lightly browned.

TO SERVE
Turn the cheesecake out on to a serving plate, scatter over the
pea shoots and flowers. Nestle the Parmesan crisps among
them. Serve warm, with a crispy and peppery side salad.

GROW
Garlic (see page 168)
Lemon (see page 119)
Peas (see page 158)
Viola flowers
(see page 125)

POTATOES

Potatoes have long been included in baking, to add both moisture and bulk to savoury and sweet cakes and breads. When used out of choice rather than necessity, it makes sense to grow the varieties that will impart the best flavour.

BAKE
Ginger cake (see page 87)
Pesto potato scones
(see facing page)

BEST VARIETIES

The early and salad potatoes work well for baking, as they have a lower water content than larger maincrop varieties. 'International Kidney' is the closest a home-grower can get to a 'Jersey Royal' new potato, while 'Epicure' is another good early and salad 'Pink Fir Apple' has a great flavour. 'Cara' and 'Arran Victory' are more good choices.

PLANTING

Potatoes develop from specially grown seed potatoes, which are available to buy from late winter. These should be put in a cool, dry, light place to chit (the formation of little leafy sprouts out of the seed potato) – old egg boxes are ideal receptacles for this. Plant out the chitted potatoes in early spring, putting them sprout-end up in a hole three times their depth and covering carefully so as not to damage the young shoots. Space the plants 30cm/12in apart, with 40cm/16in between rows. To encourage the formation of more potatoes, once the shoots reach about 10cm/4in above the surface, cover them over with soil drawn up from either side of the row.

To plant in deep pots or sacks, put a 15cm/6in tier of compost in the bottom of the pot, place the chitted potatoes on top and cover with another 30cm/12in of compost. Cover the shoots when they break through as above until you reach the top of the pot/sack.

MAINTENANCE

Protect the leaves from frost with horticultural fleece, newspaper or cardboard. Water only in dry weather, as otherwise watering encourages the development of more leaves than potatoes.

HARVEST

Potatoes will be ready to harvest 3–5 months after planting, depending on whether they are early or maincrop varieties. Make sure you dig up all the potatoes, even the very little ones; any remaining may develop into more plants there next year.

BELOW Earth up potatoes by drawing up the soil from the sides of the rows.

PESTO POTATO SCONES

MAKES 10–12 SCONES

YOU WILL NEED
- 1 × baking sheet, dusted with flour
- 1 × cookie cutter, 6cm/2½in diameter

INGREDIENTS

For the pesto:
- 65g/2oz basil leaves
- 1 garlic clove, crushed
- 13g/½oz pine nuts
- small pinch of salt
- 60ml/2fl oz olive oil
- 50g/2oz Parmesan cheese, finely grated

For the scones:
- 2 eggs, beaten
- 300g/10oz potatoes, boiled, drained and mashed
- 300g/10oz plain flour
- 1 tbsp baking powder
- ½ tsp salt

Although the potatoes add a depth of flavour, as well as moisture to replace the need for butter and milk, these scones are really about the pesto. Making your own pesto is a viable option only if you grow your own basil, as it is needed in quantity. It is well worth having a basil plant – or several – to hand. In winter try substituting parsley for the basil and walnuts for the pine nuts.

METHOD
- **For the pesto**, blend all the ingredients except the cheese into a consistent paste, then stir in the cheese and set aside.
- **For the scones**, preheat the oven to 180°C/350°F/gas mark 4. Mash the eggs into the cooled potato with a fork, then sift in the flour, baking powder and salt. Mash roughly, then add 150g/5oz of the pesto and bring it all together to a dough. Tip the dough out on to a floured surface and flatten to around 3cm/1¼in thick. Punch out the scones using the cookie cutter and place on the floured tray. Reshape the dough and continue cutting out the scones. Bake for 20–25 minutes until risen and slightly browned. Remove from the oven and cool on a wire rack for 5–10 minutes.

TO SERVE
Serve warm, slathered with cold butter.

GROW
Basil (see page 109)
Garlic (see page 168)
Potatoes
(see facing page)

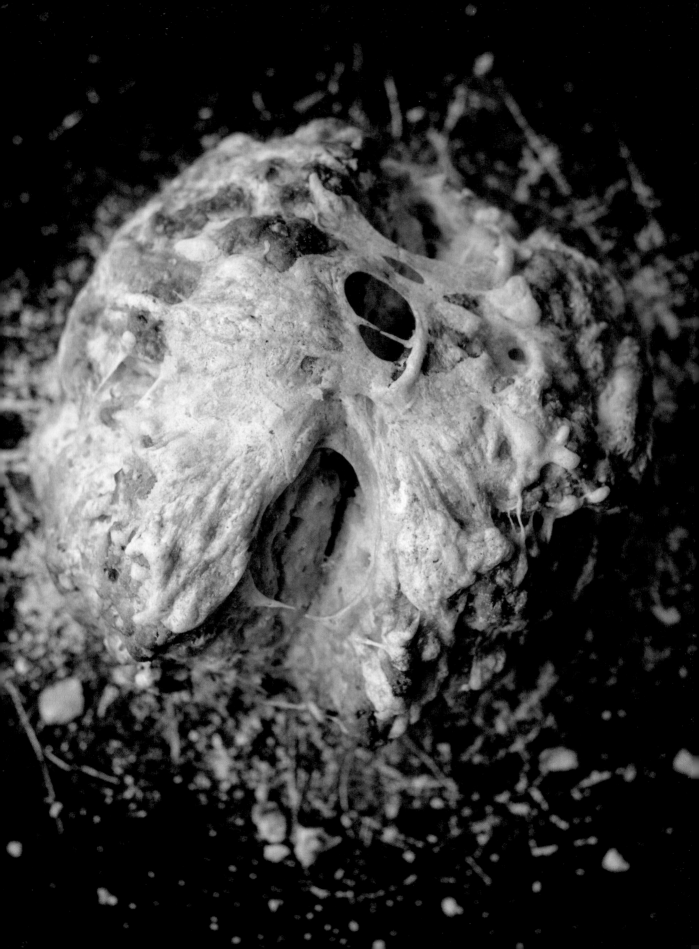

PUMPKIN SODA BREAD

MAKES 2 LOAVES

YOU WILL NEED
1 × baking sheet,
dusted with flour

INGREDIENTS
500g/1lb 2oz plain flour,
    plus extra for dusting
1 tsp salt
pinch of freshly ground pepper
4 tsp baking powder
150g/5oz grated pumpkin
100g/3½oz grated
    gruyere cheese
300ml/½ pint buttermilk

Soda bread, which is created using baking powder rather than yeast, requires no kneading and no proving. It is best served warm, making it an ideal choice for a quick weekend lunch. Tradition has it that the cross sliced into the top of the bread is to ward off the devil, but whatever the origin it makes each loaf easy to tear apart into chunks to share.

METHOD

- Preheat the oven to 200°C/400°F/gas mark 6. Mix the flour, salt, pepper, baking powder, pumpkin and three-quarters of the cheese quickly and thoroughly in a large bowl. Then make a well in the centre.
- Pour in the buttermilk and stir until it comes together as one ball of dough. Work as quickly as possible until the ingredients are all incorporated, but do not mix for longer than necessary to do this.
- Divide the dough into two equal pieces, and shape each into a ball. Put on to the baking sheet and flatten slightly. Cut a deep (almost to the base) cross in each ball, sprinkle with the remaining cheese and dust with a little flour.
- Bake for 25–30 minutes, until the bread sounds hollow when tapped on the base. Remove from the oven and cool on a wire rack.

TO SERVE
Serve warm or cold. The loaves will last 2 days at most, and are best eaten as soon as possible after baking.

GROW
Pumpkins &
winter squashes
(see page 84)

SPINACH

BAKE
Spinach & cheese muffins
(see facing page)

Leafy crops are some of the best to grow rather than buy, as they really benefit from being eaten as soon as possible after picking. Spinach, which can be harvested over a long period, is worth making space for in the veg patch.

BEST VARIETIES

'Amazon' and 'Palco' are both good for baby leaves and have some resistance to bolting. 'Atlanta' will withstand colder temperatures and last longer into the autumn and winter.

PLANTING

Spinach plants will happily grow in a little shade, and this will help prevent them bolting in hot weather. The plants are hardy, and can be sown in early spring. A sowing in late spring will give leaves later into autumn. Sow in drills 20cm/8in apart, thinning plants to 5–10cm/2–4in apart, for baby leaves. For bigger leaves, sow seeds 15cm/6in apart in drills 30cm/12in apart. Sow three seeds to a 30cm/12in pot.

MAINTENANCE

Regular harvesting will ensure the plants flourish. Water well; especially in hot weather keep the soil consistently moist to stave off bolting. It may be necessary to protect plants from birds, slugs and snails.

HARVEST

Start picking the leaves as soon as they are a usable size. Regular picking of young leaves will keep the plant producing fresh crops of tender leaves, but pick a few leaves from each plant rather than denuding a single one entirely. Older leaves will be tougher and more bitter.

RIGHT Always rinse spinach before using, to wash off any soil and grit particles.

SPINACH & CHEESE MUFFINS

These flavourful muffins are just the thing to sustain you through the afternoon on the allotment or in the garden.

MAKES 12 MUFFINS

YOU WILL NEED

1 × 12-hole muffin or cupcake tin, lined with paper cases

INGREDIENTS

Spinach mix:
15g/½oz unsalted butter
½ shallot, finely chopped
1 garlic clove, finely chopped
250g/8oz spinach, roughly chopped
small pinch of freshly grated nutmeg

Muffin batter:
375g/13oz plain flour
3 tsp baking powder
large pinch of salt
large pinch of freshly ground pepper
150g/5oz cheddar cheese, grated
2 eggs
375ml/13fl oz milk (semi-skimmed or full fat)
10g/½oz oats, for decoration

METHOD

- **For the spinach mix**, melt the butter in a large frying pan over a low heat, add the shallot and garlic and fry gently until softened but not coloured. Tip in the spinach, and add the nutmeg. Cook, stirring, until the spinach has completely wilted and reduced. There should be hardly any liquid left. Leave to cool, then roughly chop again.
- **For the muffin batter**, preheat the oven to 180°C/350°F/gas mark 4. Sift together the flour, baking powder, salt and pepper into a large bowl, then stir in the cheese. In a separate bowl, lightly whisk the eggs into the milk. Stir the milk/egg mix into the dry ingredients until fully incorporated, then quickly fold in the spinach mix so that it is evenly distributed. Spoon into the paper cases, and sprinkle the tops with the oats. Bake for 25 minutes, then remove from the oven and turn out to cool on a wire rack.

TO SERVE

Serve warm or cold.

GROW

Garlic (see page 168)
Spinach
(see facing page)

GARLIC

Garlic, a base flavour in so many dishes, is one of the lowest-maintenance vegetables. Growing your own also means you can try plaiting the dried bulbs together into a long string to hang in the kitchen.

BAKE

Pea cheesecake (see page 160)
Pesto potato scones (see page 163)
Root veg tarte Tatin
(see facing page)
Spinach & cheese muffins
(see page 167)

BEST VARIETIES

Choose hardneck varieties (rather than softneck – the other main type of garlic), as not only do they produce better-sized cloves, but they may also put out a flower spike (known as a scape), which is edible too. Try 'Lautrec Wight' or 'Red Sicilian'. 'Elephant' garlic is not a true garlic yet produces enormous bulbs of a milder flavour: try them in the root veg tarte Tatin (see facing page).

PLANTING

Garlic needs an open, sunny site and well-drained soil, as otherwise it can be prone to rotting. It is best grown from cloves rather than seed. Bulbs (specifically for planting, although it is possible to use those sold for eating) are available from late summer, for planting in autumn and winter. Garlic requires a cold spell in order to produce plenty of cloves, so any cloves planted in spring will not divide up so well if at all. Plant the cloves direct into the ground or in a modular tray in a cold frame for transplanting in spring. Push the cloves into the soil so that they are completely covered, with the baseplate downwards (pointy end up!), leaving about 15cm/6in between cloves and 30cm/12in between rows. To grow in pots, make sure the cloves have enough space to develop into decent-sized bulbs; 6–8 plants per pot of 30cm/12in diameter is sufficient.

MAINTENANCE

Aside from keeping the weeds down, and watering in very dry weather, there's little else to do but wait. If the plants start to grow flower spikes, cut these off.

HARVEST

Garlic is ready when the leaves start to yellow and dry out in late spring or early summer; check the bulbs are big enough by lifting one. Leave the bulbs to dry out in the sun while raised off the ground, to enable good air circulation. Once the skins rustle to the touch, the bulbs can be stored in a cool, dry place.

RIGHT Plant garlic cloves with the basal plate downwards.

ROOT VEG TARTE TATIN

SERVES 2 AS A MAIN COURSE

YOU WILL NEED

1 × flan tin, 20cm/8in diameter, greased and base-lined

INGREDIENTS

250g/8oz puff pastry
300–400g/10–14oz
    root vegetables
15g/½oz unsalted butter
1 tbsp fresh herbs, finely
    chopped (thyme and
    rosemary work well with
    all the veg)
salt and pepper, to taste
vinaigrette (optional),
    for drizzling

This is a versatile and easy dish that can include any type of root vegetable. Tarte Tatin is baked upside-down, and the vegetables are arranged on the bottom of the tin so that when turned out they are in an attractive pattern on the pastry – get creative with the shapes and colours of your veg! (NB By all means make your own puff pastry, but to make this bake easier and faster I would recommend using shop-bought – just make sure it is all-butter pastry.)

This tart is especially good with thinnings or baby vegetables of carrots, beetroot and parsnips: use just one type of vegetable per tarte Tatin, or mix several together. Use baby veg and thinnings whole, cut full-sized roots into small chunks or slices. Roasting garlic (especially 'Elephant' garlic) makes it creamy and mild flavoured.

GROW

Beetroot (see page 58)
Carrots (see page 50)
Garlic (see facing page)
Parsnips (see page 94)
Rosemary (see page 110)
Thyme (see page 111)

METHOD

- Roll out the pastry and cut out a disc of 22cm/8½in diameter (that is, just bigger than the base of the tin). Wrap in baking paper and put in the refrigerator.
- Preheat the oven to 180°C/350°F/gas mark 4. Arrange the prepared vegetables in the base of the tin, remembering that the underside will be what is on display once served. Dot over the butter, sprinkle with three-quarters of the herbs and season well with salt and pepper. Cover the top of the tin with foil and bake for 20–40 minutes until the vegetables are tender.
- Remove from the oven and take off the foil. Turn the oven up to 190°C/375°F/gas mark 5. Take the pastry disc out of the refrigerator and place it over the top of the vegetables. Tuck the edges down the sides. Return the tin to the oven and bake for a further 20 minutes until the pastry is puffed up and golden. Remove from the oven and leave to cool in the tin for 10 minutes.

TO SERVE

Turn out, inverted, on to a serving board. Peel off the base paper, scatter with the remaining chopped herbs and drizzle with a vinaigrette, if liked.

USEFUL FURTHER INFORMATION

MORE INFORMATION

The Royal Horticultural Society has a wealth of growing information on its website, including advice on pruning fruit trees and dealing with pests and diseases: www.rhs.org.uk.

RHS Vegetable and Fruit Gardening (ed. Michael Pollock, Dorling Kindersley, 2012) is an all-encompassing tome on growing your own.

RHS New Encyclopaedia of Herbs and Their Uses (Deni Brown, Dorling Kindersley, 2002) contains all you will ever need to know about growing and using herbs and edible flowers.

RHS Grow for Flavour (James Wong, Mitchell Beazley, 2015) contains a number of useful tips on maximizing the flavour of your home-grown produce.

RECOMMENDED SUPPLIERS

Blackmoor Nurseries for fruit trees and plants: www.blackmoor.co.uk

Chiltern Seeds for vegetable, herb and flower seeds: www.chilternseeds.co.uk

Otter Farm for the usual and more unusual crops as plants or seeds: www.otterfarm.co.uk

Sea Spring Seeds for vegetable and chilli seeds: www.seaspringseeds.co.uk

You can contact me through my website, www.hollyefarrell.com, or twitter, @Holly_E_Farrell.

LEFT Citrus trees can flower all year round and have a delicious perfume.

INDEX

Page numbers in *italics* indicate a caption to an illustration; those in **bold**, boxed text.
Ingredients included in a recipe but obviously not a main ingredient, e.g. flour, are not indexed.

ACKNOWLEDGMENTS

I have, I hope, been effusive in my thanks to the people who made this book happen, but I record them here again. Once more with feeling . . .

Jason Ingram, it was a privilege and a lot of fun to work with you on this book. Thank you for making everything look so wonderful and for keeping in good humour despite having to work with both children and animals.

Becky Clarke brought the book to life with her lovely designs and my editor Joanna Chisholm kept my prose tethered to the ground. Thank you both for your hard work and patience.

Obviously this book would not have come about without the good people of Frances Lincoln – I am extremely grateful to Helen Griffin and Andrew Dunn for giving me this opportunity in the first place, and for their ambition for the project.

Rupert and Liz Lywood, thank you for your generosity. Thank you also to Mark Diacono, Great British Florist, Wild Bunch and the Ludlow Cookshop.

I am very grateful to Tracey Tyler, Alison Hedges, Melissa Jeacock, Mia Munnerley and Sue Moss for volunteering to test the recipes.

When the man who was to become my husband first tried my baking, he nearly choked, the scones were so dry (in my defence, they were five days old). I doubt he thought then that I would – should! – ever write a baking book. I certainly did not. That it should now come to pass is due in large part to his support and encouragement. Kevin, my inspiration and my chief taster, thank you.

PICTURE CREDITS

All images are copyright © Jason Ingram except for the following:
GAP: 17 © Elke Borkowski (#0208400); 54 © Michael King (#0385705)
Shutterstock: 64 © yuris; 74 © CGissemann; 80 © Auhustsinovich; 87 © Jojoo64; 108 © Paul Maguire